Making
Screw
Threads
in Wood

Making
Screw
Threads
in Wood

Fred Holder

Guild of Master Craftsman Publications

First published 2001 by

Guild of Master Craftsman Publications Ltd,

166 High Street, Lewes,

East Sussex, BN7 1XU

Cover photo of Allan Beecham hand-chasing a thread by Anthony Bailey

Illustrations by Simon Rodway

ISBN 1 86108 195 2

A catalogue record of this book is available from the British Library

Designed by John Hawkins

Typeface: Palatino

Colour origination by Viscan Graphics (Singapore)

Printed in Hong Kong by H&Y Printing Ltd

This book would never have been written without the inspiration provided by Bill Jones' articles in the UK magazine *Woodturning*. Bill so casually mentioned cutting threads using a hand-held chaser, it stimulated me to study and learn this ancient method for producing screw threads in wood, and without this, I probably wouldn't have developed such an interest in the various other methods available for making threads in wood.

Much of this book could not have been written had it not been for the companies that manufacture tools for making threads in wood. This is especially true for the various thread-cutting jigs on the market today. The first that I heard about was the Bonnie Klein Threading Jig, designed to work on her Klein Design Lathe. Next I discovered the SG-400, sold by Craft Supplies Ltd, and then the Nova Ornamental Turner, manufactured by Teknatool International in New Zealand. Then, just before this book was completed, the Beall Masterpiece Turner came onto the market allowing me to make the work as current as possible.

Finally, I must acknowledge the encouragement of my late wife, Arlene, who urged me to undertake the task, and especially Stephanie Horner of GMC Publications who also encouraged and stimulated me to write this book.

Note on measurements

For chasing screw threads, metric and imperial designations are not compatible. An imperial thread size is always given as the number of threads per inch while the thread pitch is given for a metric thread size. Further, you cannot use a chaser set up to cut a number of threads per inch to cut any particular metric thread and vice versa. For these reasons conversions of screw thread measurements between metric and imperial are not appropriate, and they have not been given in this book.

Introduction

The invention of the screw thread has been lost in history, there are simply artifacts from times past which contain screw threads, proving that they did exist. Though it is not clear exactly when screw threads came into use, it is thought that the earliest examples were hand cut in wood and that they did not have a matching internal thread, but instead, a follower that rode in the thread cut in a spindle. It is very likely that these early screw threads were fairly coarse, used to position pieces on a machine, to lift such items as lamps, or to press such things as grapes and olives. In some cases they may simply have been used for decoration.

But this book is not about the past. It is designed to help you understand screw threads and how they can be made in wood, thus, hopefully, removing much of the mystic surrounding this operation. Part One covers the various techniques available and Part Two applies these to specific projects, each designed to illustrate a particular way of using threads in wood.

Although most wood screw threads are cut on a lathe, I also address the use of taps and screw boxes to cut threads by hand: you do not have to be a machinist or a skilled lathe operator to cut threads in wood.

Techniques

Allan Beecham hand-chasing a thread

Chapter 1

About screw threads

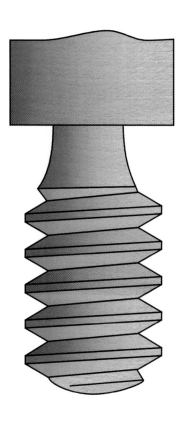

It is likely that the earliest screws in history were made in wood and hand carved using a knife or chisel, or perhaps a broken rock with a sharp edge. The earliest forms of screw threads may have been purely for decoration, perhaps cut between the strips of rawhide that were wrapped around tool and weapon handles. Someone may have learned, by chance, that by mounting such a cylinder, with its spiralling groove, between two points, a follower could be added to move something along the spiral. This may have been the first use of the screw. Unfortunately this is all speculation, as we have no written records of the actual invention of the screw.

The earliest record I've been able to find dates to around 200BC, when the Greek mathematician Apollonius described the geometry of a spiral helix, which is the basis for a screw thread. Greeks and Romans both used screw presses to squeeze grapes and crush olives. A Pompeiian mural is believed to show a screw press being used to make linen.

Laying out a screw thread

A screw thread can be laid out by wrapping a tapered piece of paper around a cylinder; the edge of the paper represents the centre line of the screw thread and gives a continuous and uniform angle to the screw line (see Fig 1.1). The actual threads per inch that a particular taper will generate is determined by the angle of the taper and the circumference of the cylinder. A strip of tape or a strip of paper cut to a uniform width may also be wrapped around a cylinder, with the angle of wrap set so that the next wrap lays perfectly against the previous wrap (see Fig 1.2). The width of the paper or tape is then the 'pitch' of the thread. The edge of the tape corresponds to the top of the ridge of the screw thread. This technique can be used to lay out a screw thread to be carved by hand.

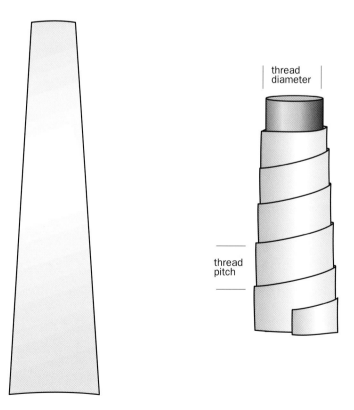

Fig 1.1 When a tapered strip of paper is wrapped around a cylinder, the taper of the wedge and the diameter of the cylinder determine the thread pitch

thread diameter

thread pitch

Fig 1.2
Generating a
spiral by wrapping
a strip of paper
around a cylinder

Coarse threads can be laid out by marking directly onto the cylinder in the same manner as laying out a spiral on wood, especially if you have the wood mounted in a lathe. It requires four equally spaced lines around the cylinder for each complete revolution of the spiral. As a spiral generally makes one complete revolution over several inches of the cylinder this is not a problem; however, a screw thread tends to make several revolutions over just one inch, so it is more difficult to lay out screw threads in this way. For example, to lay out one revolution of the thread, with the cylinder mounted horizontally, you must measure out a space on the cylinder equivalent to one inch divided by the number of threads per inch; a two-thread per inch thread would make one revolution around the cylinder in ½in of horizontal travel (see Fig 1.3). To lay out this thread in the fashion used for spirals, you must divide ½in of the cylinder into four sections, each ⅛in wide. You must then divide the circumference of the cylinder into quadrants. These quadrants and the initial four division lines create four rectangles that are one-quarter of the circumference of the cylinder in length and ⅛in wide.

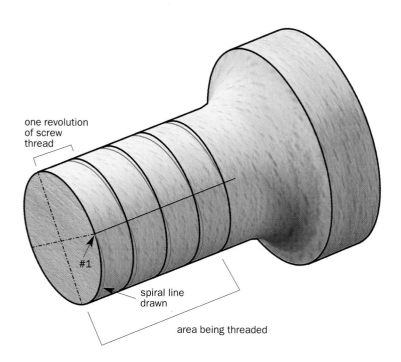

Fig 1.3 Laying out a 2tpi screw thread with a pitch of ½in

one revolution of screw thread

#1

spiral line drawn

area being threaded

Take a pencil or other marking device and, beginning at the right-hand edge of the ½in section where one of the quadrant lines intersects with it (we'll call this #1), draw a diagonal line from the lower right-hand corner to the upper left-hand corner of the rectangle. You now have the beginning of the thread. Move to the next ⅛in section and the next quadrant. The line you just drew stopped at the lower right-hand corner of this new rectangle. Draw another diagonal line from here to the upper left-hand corner. Continue this on around the cylinder until a complete revolution has been made. This procedure will make a single-start thread. Often, on large screws of this type, a thread start is made on each of the quadrants so that there are actually four parallel screw threads moving around the cylinder.

As you can see, this will be a near impossible task with more threads per inch. However, for coarse threads as described here, it is quite reasonable to lay out the threads on a cylinder and cut them by hand using a saw, chisel, and file.

Cutting internal threads

It is fairly easy to use one of the above methods to lay out your coarse screw threads on a large diameter cylinder and to carve them by hand. Cutting internal threads for a nut to ride on this screw is another thing. It is a near impossible task to execute. The normal practice, therefore, was to have a follower ride in the screw thread to move along the thread as the cylinder was rotated. This follower generally fit the shape of the screw thread and was angled to match the rate of progression. The screw that brought the paper down onto the type on the Gutenberg Printing Press was an application of this type of screw (see Fig 1.4). When used in this way it was not unusual to use a four-start screw.

Screw-thread design

I mention all of this simply to give you some idea of how screw threads actually work. They are a continuous, uniform spiral around a cylinder and may range from very coarse threads per inch, in heavy industrial machinery, to very fine threads per inch, in precision instruments such as watches. In the early days, each manufacturer tended to make their own thread design so that customers had to return to them for replacement parts when their machine broke down or a part or screw were lost. Gradually, some standards began to emerge so that if you had a particular screw thread you could buy a replacement part with the same screw thread without having to return to the manufacturer to have a part manufactured for you.

It has never been common to buy wooden screw threads in the hardware store as screw threads in wood are generally pretty design specific. However, there are some mix-and-match furniture components available that do come with threaded parts

and you can buy individual replacements for these. Broom handles, among other things, can be bought as replacement parts if the original handle is broken. These carry threaded joins so that they can be screwed into the broom head.

Fig 1.4 This model of the Gutenberg Printing Press uses a large wooden screw to apply pressure during printing

Taps and dies

Threads in wood were perhaps even less standardized than those in metal. Often a blacksmith was charged with the task of making a tap to cut the internal threads and a die, or screw box, to cut matching external threads. These would vary from place to place depending upon how the blacksmith made the original tap. To illustrate this type of operation, I would like to quote from *Practical Blacksmithing*, edited by M. T. Richardson, circa 1889–1891. (Refer to Fig 1.5 for the Fig references in the following quote.)

'To make wooden screws by my plan, first take a square piece of steel and with a three-cornered file make the thread on all four corners of the steel for about two inches. When this is done you will have a tap as seen in Fig 187.

'To make the screw box as shown in Fig 188, turn a piece of wood (apple wood is best), with two handles, and bore a hole in the center to the size of the tap with the thread off. Then cut a thread in it with the tap and cut away the wood at one side to admit the knife. This is made as in Fig 189 with two screws in it, one in the center and the other to set it.

'Put the knife in the box so it will match the thread, and screw in over it a piece of wood one-quarter of an inch thick with a hole in it the size of the tap with the thread on, as represented in Fig 190. The box is then complete. (H.A.S.)'

This was a fairly typical way to make threads in wood in the late 1800s. This technique would be used in furniture making or any instance where wooden threads were needed. As tools and equipment became more standardized, taps to cut the internal threads became commercially available, as did thread boxes and dies with matching threads.

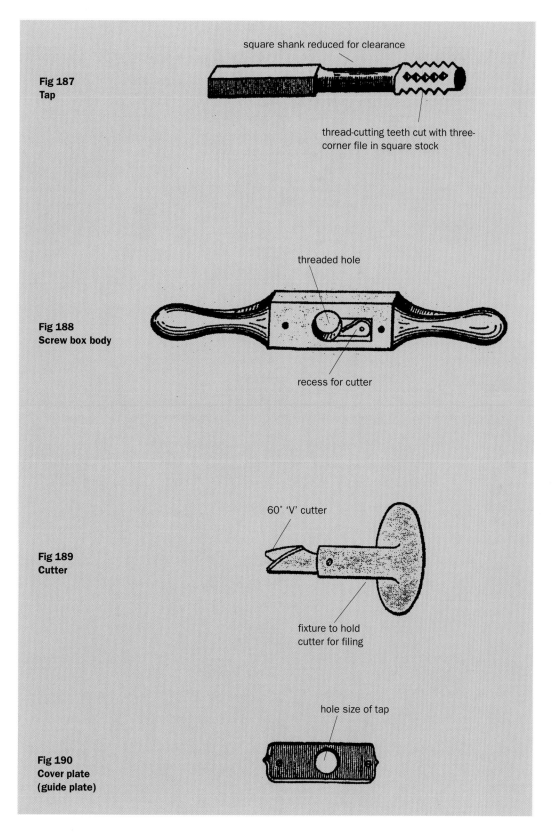

square shank reduced for clearance

Fig 187
Tap

thread-cutting teeth cut with three-corner file in square stock

threaded hole

Fig 188
Screw box body

recess for cutter

60° 'V' cutter

Fig 189
Cutter

fixture to hold cutter for filing

hole size of tap

Fig 190
Cover plate (guide plate)

The use of taps and dies presents two problems:

1   you need a large number of taps and dies in order to cover a range of size requirements; and

2   the taps and dies do not always start exactly straight, hence the two pieces do not necessarily screw together straight.

You can buy sets of taps and dies for metal, containing both fine and coarse threads, from about ⅛–½in, in ¹⁄₁₆in increments. However, as they are designed for use in metals they don't work as well for woods. They will work fairly well for the hard, dense woods such as lignum vitae, African blackwood and boxwood, but for the softer hardwoods, coarser threads are generally desired because of their greater strength. Such threads are found in taps and dies specifically designed for use in wood. Most of them are available in coarse threads and in sizes of ½, ¾, 1in and up. Some of the most common uses for these are screw-in legs for furniture, handles for brooms, and handles for gavels, etc.

Lathes

Because specific sizes of tenon are required in order to use taps and dies, the lathe has been a favourite choice for making threads in both metal and wood. In this book we are concerned solely with making threads in wood.

In harder woods, which are able to hold a standard metal screw thread, the wood lathe and the hand-held chaser are the quickest and easiest ways to cut threads. You could also use a metal lathe, but if you only need one set of threads, the set-up time is prohibitive. With hand-held chasers you could have the job done and be on to something else faster than you could get the metal lathe set up to cut threads.

This box, made from spalted maple, was threaded using a lathe with a threading jig

As hand-held chasers are scraping tools, they will not work successfully on the softer hardwoods. On these it is better to use one of the thread-cutting jigs on a lathe. These are specifically designed for use on the wood lathe and have a primary use of cutting threads for threaded boxes, but they also work nicely making such things as bolts and screw-on finials.

Thread chasers

A thread chaser is a scraping tool. It works well on the very hard woods but tends to tear chunks out of softer woods, just as any scraper might do. Thread-cutting jigs hold the wood in a chuck to rotate and move it forward at the proper rate while a high-speed cutter cuts the groove in the wood. This allows the cutting of threads in much softer woods than could be cut with a hand-held chaser.

All screw threads have three main characteristics: form, diameter and pitch (see Fig 1.6). Threads in both imperial and metric systems use the 60° form (an equilateral triangle). The two characteristics of any thread that are different are diameter and pitch. In the imperial system, a thread is specified by the diameter and the number of threads per inch (tpi). For example, ¾in x 16tpi means that the diameter is ¾in and there are 16 threads per inch. The pitch is determined by the number of threads per inch; where there are 16 threads per inch, the pitch will be ⅟₁₆in.

In the metric system, now used in much of the world, a thread is specified by the diameter and the pitch. As an example, a metric designation of 24 x 2 means that the outside diameter is 24mm and each thread completes a full revolution in 2mm. A metric thread chaser would be gauged in this fashion, ie, the designation would be the distance between the points on the chaser as measured in millimetres.

All of the thread chasers that I've seen use the threads per inch designation and have the 60° form. However, while I haven't seen any thread chasers made for the metric

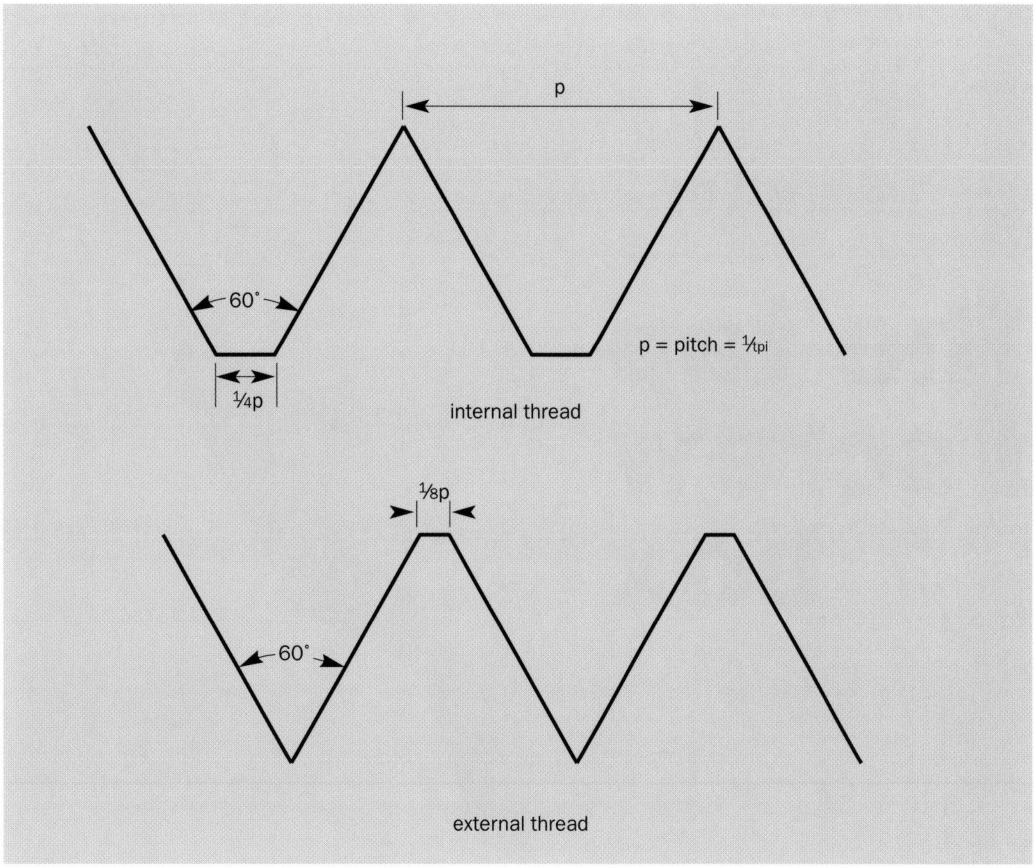
p
60°
¼p
p = pitch = 1/tpi
internal thread
⅛p
60°
external thread

Fig 1.6 The configuration of internal and external threads. Note that both have flats on the top of the thread. This is extremely important on wood threads, as pointed threads are easily broken

system as yet, some of the threading jigs for use with wood lathes come in metric. It would simplify things if the whole world were to adopt the metric system, but it would likely take another hundred years or more to completely abolish the use of the imperial system, which is still used extensively in America, because of the time it would take for tools and equipment to wear out.

Chapter 2

The tap and screw box

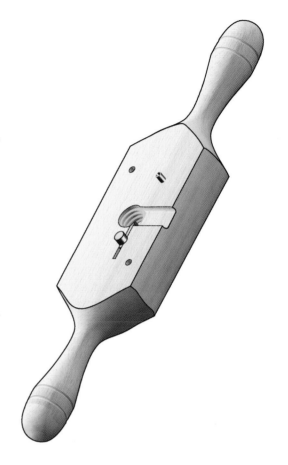

In Chapter 1 I talked about the various methods of cutting threads in wood. One method briefly described was the use of a tap to cut the internal threads and a screw box to cut the external threads (see Fig 2.1). This method works fairly well with cylinders about ½–3in in diameter. Above 3in it becomes cumbersome and below ½in it is very difficult to get a strong enough external thread on a wooden dowel. However, internal threads can often be made in wood using regular metalworking taps and metal screws can then be used to screw into these holes. For internal threads it is best if the grain of the wood is at 90° to the centre line of the hole so that the threads contain some end grain and some side grain, thus giving a stronger thread. When using machinist's taps, always use the coarsest thread available for that diameter of hole: in wood coarser threads are always a bit stronger.

Making the tap

To use these tools properly it helps to understand how they are made. The tap must be made of steel. If you are only going to use it occasionally or are making it for a specific job, you don't need to use hardened steel, but if you will be using the tap often, you should make it from high carbon steel annealed to its softest state so that you can file it to shape. Once you have it shaped and have cut the thread into it, with a file, it needs to be heat-treated to harden and temper it. Since few woodworkers are blacksmiths, I'll not tell you how to heat-treat your tap. That task is best left to the professionals. Actually, the making of the tap is really best left to the professional blacksmith, though it is well within the capabilities of the average experienced craftsman.

The stock for the tap should be tapered on the end so that the finished tap is tapered: this makes it easier to start the hole. Of course, it presents a problem if you need to tap a blind hole (one that does not go all the way through the wood). This is why

Fig 2.1
A commercial screw box and taps. One tap is the normal threading tap, with a tapered end to simplify starting a thread. The other is a bottoming tap, which is used to take threads near the bottom of a blind hole

most commercially made taps come in two forms: a tapered tap for tapping holes that do go right through the wood or for *starting* blind holes, and a bottoming tap for finishing the threading just to the bottom of the hole.

The Beall Tool Company circumvented this problem by making their taps with a removable guide so that blind holes can be properly bottomed. This guide slides into the drilled hole and aligns the tap properly for starting the threading, thus removing the need for a tapered tap. Unless you have a metalworker's lathe and good metalworking experience, I suggest you leave such sophistication to the experts.

Once you have the tap blank properly sized, you need to cut chip grooves that run the full length of the threaded area. If the threaded area is larger than the shaft that will be used to turn it, this can be done fairly easily with a triangular file or a small round file. I find the round file best for finishing these grooves. I don't know whether they are any more functional, but they do look better. At least four grooves should be cut, but you can make more or less and still have a functional tap.

The next decision you need to make is what pitch you want for your threads. Pitch is the distance between peaks on the thread. You can use finer threads – ie less pitch – in the very hard woods, such as African blackwood and boxwood, than you can in softer woods like maple.

In his book, *The Woodwright's Work Book*, Roy Underhill states that the 'perfect pitch' is $\frac{1}{12}$ of the circumference of the piece being threaded. He further states that anything finer than $\frac{1}{18}$ of the circumference will make the threads too fragile. Roy's definition results in some pretty coarse threads. For example, a $\frac{1}{2}$in diameter dowel would have a pitch of $\frac{1}{8}$in and would result in a thread of about 7.6 to the inch. Although this seems pretty coarse for such a small diameter, the threads would be fairly strong even in softer woods.

This maple box was threaded with 6¾tpi threads using the Beall Masterpiece Turner

If we use Roy's criteria, the easy way to proceed in laying out the threads is to cut a piece of paper as long as the threaded section and as wide as the circumference of the tap, ie if the paper is wrapped around the tap, its ends should just meet. Now, if you set out dividers so that they are exactly $\frac{1}{12}$ of the circumference and make step marks along each joining edge of the paper for the full length of the thread, you will have the beginning of a thread layout. Using a ruler, draw a line from the top corner of one side to the first step mark on the other. Continue in this way down the paper, drawing lines parallel to this, from the next mark on the first side, to the next mark on the second.

Wrap the paper around the area of thread and make sure the lines join. If all is well, glue the paper to the area of the tap to be threaded and then, using a hacksaw and a triangular file, cut between the lines to create the threads. This file work should produce a 60° groove that spirals around the tap for the full length of the threads, with the peak of the threads just eliminating the line. The start of the threads should have a slight taper to allow the tap to engage easily.

I've described how to make the tap for those hardy souls who wish to do the whole thing themselves or who wish to create a set of threads different from anything available on the market. Personally, I recommend buying a tap and matching screw box for threading. They are readily available and the development problems have already been worked out for you. If you do choose to make your own, you must make the tap first as you will need it to make the screw box.

Making the screw box

A screw box is made up of two blocks of wood. The main block has integral handles and a threaded hole through its centre, with the other block, the guide plate, attached to its bottom. The guide plate has a hole of the same diameter as the dowel that is to be threaded. It serves to guide the dowel accurately to the cutter at the bottom of the main box and hold it in proper alignment for threading. The hole in the guide plate must align perfectly with the threaded hole in the main block of the screw box.

Fig 2.2 Drilling the hole through the guide plate

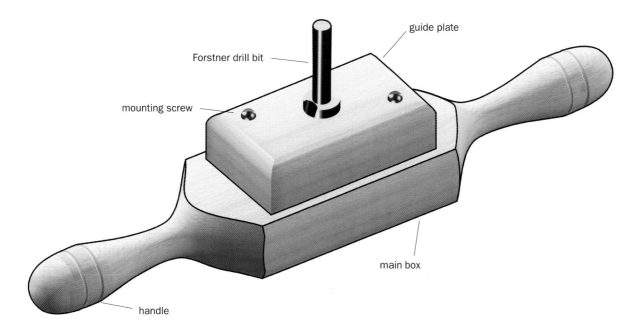

Fig 2.2 Drilling the hole through the guide plate

The two blocks should be screwed together initially for boring the holes. The larger hole should be drilled first, through the guide block, then the smaller hole drilled through the main body. You should also use the guide hole to help align the tap when tapping the threaded hole in the main body. Wood used for a screw box must be dry and hard; boxwood, fruit woods and holly should work quite well.

Having shaped the two pieces, assemble them then drill a hole through the guide plate, to the same diameter as the tap, using a Forstner drill (see Fig 2.2). Next drill a smaller hole, with a diameter the same as the root diameter of the tap, through

Fig 2.3 Tapping the hole through the main body of the screw box; note the guide plate being used to align the tap

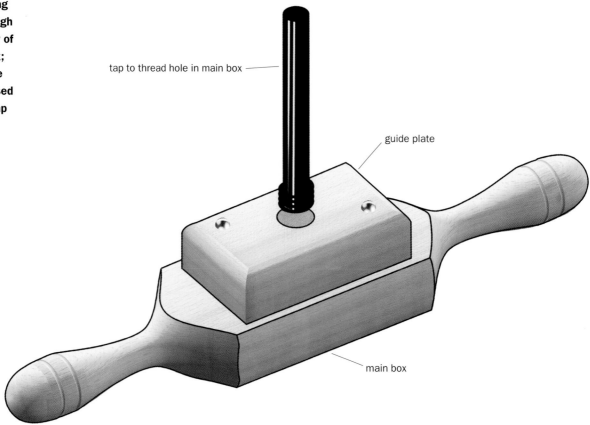

tap to thread hole in main box

guide plate

main box

the main box. Use the guide plate to help you while you thread this hole in the main block (see Fig 2.3), using the tap for which your screw box will make matching external threads.

Insert a 'V' shaped cutter into the bottom of the screw box in such a way that it aligns with the threads in the wood. This cutter is generally held in place with a couple of screws. It is important that the cutter be a good 60° 'V' cutter that matches the thread profile of the tap. The alignment of the cutter to the threads is very important because it cuts a groove into the dowel, which then enters the threaded portion of the screw box. As the newly threaded wood follows the screw threads in the screw box, it pulls the unthreaded part of the dowel into the cutter, thus cutting

Fig 2.4 The cutter
is aligned to the
threads, and a
recess cut to
allow the chips
to escape

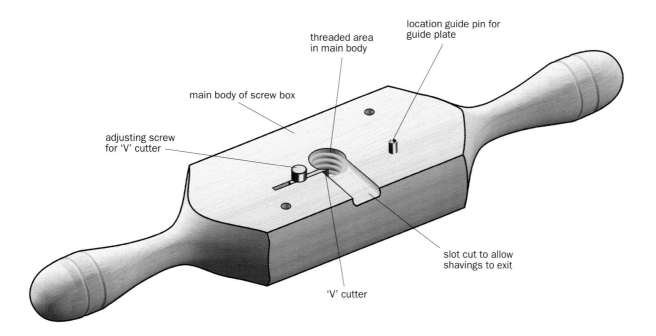

location guide pin for
guide plate

threaded area
in main body

main body of screw box

adjusting screw
for 'V' cutter

slot cut to allow
shavings to exit

'V' cutter

a spiral groove in the dowel to match the threads made by the tap. Cut a slot into the block to allow shavings from the dowels being threaded to escape (see Fig 2.4). According to Roy Underhill, the screw box will take you about as much time to make as the tap did.

The most difficult part of making a screw box is producing a proper 'V' cutter and fitting it accurately into the block so that the grooves cut into the dowel will mate properly with the threads cut into the block of wood above the cutter. The 'V' cutter must match the profile of the threads exactly. Figure 2.5 shows a cutter made from square stock. A 60° 'V' cut was made in the end, with a three-cornered file, and a bevel then ground on each side to match the 'V' cut and to provide a sharp cutting

Fig 2.5 Ideally, the cutter should be made from annealed, square-tooled steel, filed and ground to shape, then hardened and tempered to make a long-lasting cutter

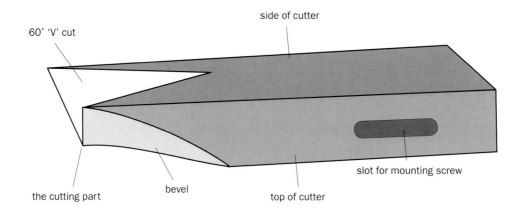

60° 'V' cut

side of cutter

slot for mounting screw

the cutting part

bevel

top of cutter

edge. If you use a single hold-down screw, cut a mounting hole that is slotted to allow for adjustment of the cutter. The cutter actually lays on its side in the main body with the slot of the mounting hole upright. It is quite possible to use a section of a 60° 'V' chisel as a cutter as long as it is sharpened properly and you can come up with a way to hold it correctly in the main body of the screw box.

This basic information will help you in making a screw box if you need one of an unusual size. Again, where possible, I recommend that you buy commercial taps and screw boxes so that you can spend your time enjoying thread cutting and other woodwork rather than making tools – unless you enjoy making the tools as much as you enjoy the woodwork.

The Beall Threader

Making large numbers of threaded pieces with a screw box could become quite tedious. To combat this, the Beall Tool Company devised their Beall Threader, which uses a rotating cutter to cut threads in a range of sizes. Power is supplied by your router and the rig comes with a table which provides a fastening point for the router and a stable positioning for the cutter with respect to the wooden dowel.

Fig 2.6 Drilling the hole for the nut. A Forstner-type drill works very well for this task. I used a ⅝in Forstner drill for this ¾in tap

The Beall Threader works in a very similar way to a screw box in that a threaded piece pulls the threaded dowel past the cutter. The advantage of the Beall Threader is that once it is set up you can cut cleaner and sharper threads than those produced by the inset 'V' cutter of the screw box – and more quickly. If you are planning to do fairly large runs of production, this is a good way to go and the Threader would pay for itself in short order. However, if you need only an occasional screw thread, it is expensive.

Cutting the threads

By this point you have likely already deduced how to make screw threads. To make internal threads you must first make a hole. The hole you drill should be the diameter of your tap's 'root diameter'. Most taps come with instructions on what

Fig 2.7 Tapping the nut using the tap with the tapered end

size drill to use. If you use too large a drill, your hole will be too large and the threads too shallow, which will weaken the threads and the holding power of the nut. Too small a drill may lead to undue stress in the wood being cut, which could cause it to split or to be overly compressed.

If the latter is the case, when the wood is allowed to relax, the grip on the bolt may become excessive and lead to a seized bolt. Neither condition is good. You want your screw threads to screw together easily without binding and have enough freedom to avoid seizing up when the weather turns damp. A tap with the proper size hole will give you that result.

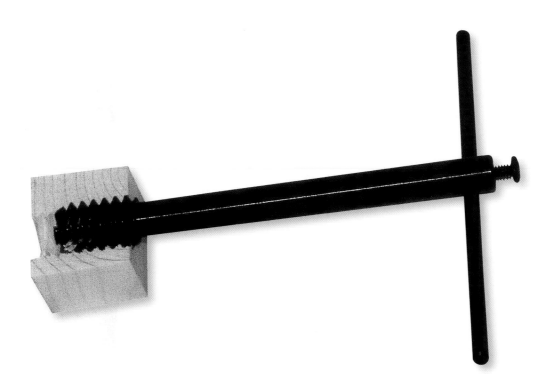

Fig 2.8 The bottoming tap shown cut away to illustrate how the tap can finish a blind hole

The tap is used to make internal threads in the nut or wherever the screw is to be attached (see Fig 2.7). It takes a fair amount of force to rotate the tap through hard, dry woods, so you will need a good 'T' handle on your tap and the wood must be attached firmly to your bench, with the hole extending over the edge of the bench or held in a vice. As you run the tap into the wood, I recommend that you cut in a short way and then back the tap out a bit. This gives the wood a slight burnish and keeps the tap from getting stuck and possibly splitting the wood. This is the process I use when cutting threads in metal. Actually, if the hole goes all the way through, this allows small chips to fall through and out of the way of the cutting edges; if it doesn't, you'll need to use a bottoming tap to tap to the bottom of the hole, but be sure to blow the chips out of the hole before you do this (see Fig 2.8).

Fig 2.9 Cutting
a thread with a
screw box. You
must use both
hands to apply
downward
pressure: this
ensures that the
cutter can bite
into the wood,
which is vital for
a clean thread

When cutting the external thread with a screw box, it is important that your cutter
is sharp so that a clean shaving is cut and ejected from the exit hole. The wood
should be clamped in a vice or other holding device to keep it from slipping.

If you have a lathe with a locking spindle and a chuck that will clamp onto the
dowel, this may be a good way to hold it. The dowel must be slightly smaller than
the lead-in hole, with just enough clearance for you to rotate it. Slip the screw box
onto the end of the dowel and rotate it clockwise (see Fig 2.9).

Enough pressure must be applied for the 'V' cutter to start cutting the wood, but as the shavings start coming out from the side of the cutter, you may be able to reduce the thrust pressure: the new thread on the dowel will then pull the dowel forward into the cutter. With a good wood and a sharp cutter, you should obtain nice clean threads on the dowel that will screw easily into the threaded hole made with the tap (see Figs 2.10 and 2.11).

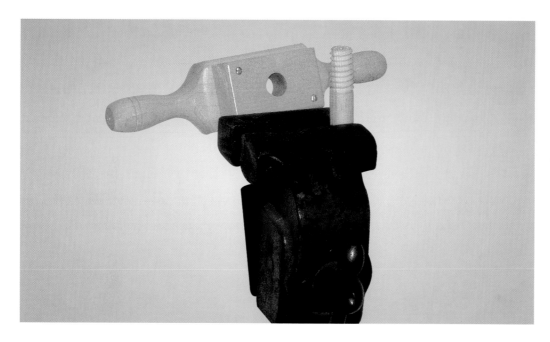

Fig 2.10
The screw box and the finished thread. This thread was cut in soft white pine to illustrate that the screw box can be used to cut threads in soft wood. However, in practice, threads in soft woods would not last very long

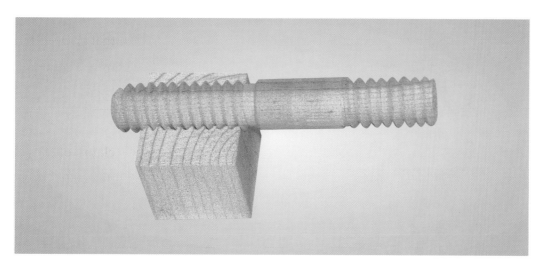

Fig 2.11 The mating of the external and internal threads cut by the tap and screw box, with the internal thread shown in cross section

Cutting threads with engineering taps and dies

Another option for cutting external threads is to use engineering taps and dies that have been designed for use on metal. I have used them successfully on the very hard woods, such as lignum vitae, boxwood, and African blackwood, but would advise against making external threads smaller than ¼in in this way, as the wood will become too fragile. It helps if the internal thread contains some end grain as well as side grain for added strength, though on the very hard woods this is not quite so important. On softer woods, such as apple and other fruit woods, I've found that tapping a hole into the wood, then flooding the threads with water-thin CA glue helps to strengthen them. (I use Red Label Hot Stuff CA glue for this.) Once the glue has set, leave for a few minutes before running the tap into the hole again to clean it up. Do not spray with accelerator, as this will cause the glue to froth up. The CA glue seems to penetrate the threads completely and give them a strength that they would otherwise not have. I have used this technique very successfully many times to make threads in knobs that will be fitted onto a No. 8 or 10 metal screw.

Using a lathe with jigs

Before the modern screw-cutting lathe was invented, there were a great number of devices and techniques used to make screw threads. Some of those techniques have been revived in the current thread-cutting jigs available for use on modern woodturning lathes. One can always use the modern metal lathe, with its many gears and power-driven tool-holder assembly, to cut threads in wood, but most woodworkers neither possess such a lathe nor have the experience to use it for cutting threads. In addition, the cutters used for metal are scraping tools and would only work on the hardest of woods such as boxwood and African blackwood. Woodworkers want something that will allow them to cut threads in almost any type of wood.

The tap and screw box described in Chapter 2 does an excellent job of threading even on very soft woods such as pine. The 'V' shaped cutter used in the screw box is essentially a 'V' shaped carving tool; when it is sharp, it will slice through even the softest of woods. The rotary cutters used so extensively on ornamental turning lathes give a clean cut in wood. Most of the threading jigs on woodturning lathes today use this type of cutter. It is mounted on the headstock spindle and rotated at a high rpm so that it cuts cleanly. Grinding the cutter to 60° causes it to cut a near perfect 60° groove for the thread. Unfortunately, these cutters still do not cut as cleanly in the softer woods as the screw box.

Threads per inch

Another factor to consider is the number of threads per inch. The screw box generally has around six or seven threads per inch, which will hold fairly well in the softer hardwoods. Most of the screw-cutting jigs cut a finer thread. The Klein Jig, for example, is available in 16 and 10tpi. The 16tpi will work well on harder woods but on the softer ones the threads will start to fall apart. Even the 10tpi is marginal on maple unless something is done to strengthen the wood, like applying thin CA glue to the wood to harden it (see page 30). Of the four jigs covered in this chapter, only the Beall Masterpiece Turner will enable you to cut threads that have a greater pitch than an 8tpi thread.

All the threading jigs covered in this chapter, with the exception of the Beall unit, mount the piece to be threaded on the spindle of the threading jig. (A very basic threading jig set-up is shown in Fig 3.1. Such a jig must be adjustable both along and across the lathe bed.) This spindle is moved back and forth by a threaded mechanism with a specific thread, for example 10tpi. By rotating the spindle, the piece to be threaded is rotated and moved forward properly so that the rotating cutter can cut a spiral that is 10tpi, regardless of the diameter of the workpiece. With these jigs, the workpiece is not limited to a specific diameter as it is with the tap and screw box, but it is limited to the number of threads per inch of the spindle. In the case of the Klein Jig, two thread sizes are available (10tpi and 16tpi).

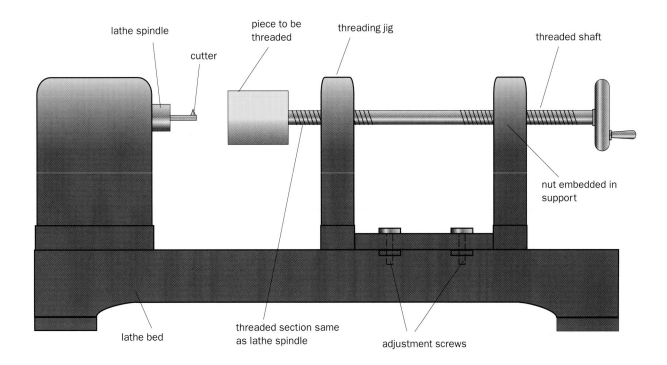

lathe spindle

cutter

piece to be threaded

threading jig

threaded shaft

nut embedded in support

threaded section same as lathe spindle

adjustment screws

lathe bed

With the Nova Ornamental Turner, three thread sizes are available (1.5mm, 2mm, and 3mm). The SG-400 has only one thread size, 2mm. The Beall Masterpiece Turner has six thread sizes available as standard set-up, however, as it uses a gearbox to establish the threads per inch, I suspect that a little experimentation will produce some additional combinations.

Fig 3.1
The general requirements of a thread-cutting jig for use on a lathe

Setting up the jig

When setting up the threading jig, it is important that the workpiece move back and forth exactly parallel to the axis of rotation of the lathe so that uniform threads are cut as the workpiece is moved into the cutter. The Klein Threading Jig is designed so that when mounted on the Klein Lathe this always happens. The centre of rotation of the threading jig's spindle and the centre of rotation of the lathe are parallel to one another. The adapters available for mounting the Klein Threading Jig to other small lathes also ensure that this parallel condition is maintained. The great flexibility of the Nova Ornamental Turner should make this a very simple set-up procedure.

The SG-400 Thread Cutting Jig and the Beall Masterpiece Turner require more effort on the part of the operator to establish this parallel condition. The jig mounts into the toolrest of the lathe and is positioned in relation to the cutter by moving the toolrest back and forth. This requires the operator to make careful visual decisions about the parallel alignment of the cutter's axis of rotation and the axis of the workpiece or the jig spindle. I haven't found this to be much of a problem; it is fairly simple to align the body of the jig visually with the bed of the lathe for both units.

Sizing

With all of these jigs there is a problem determining exactly how deep to make the threads and how to size the two pieces to be screwed together. I struggled with this problem for several years and came up with a few methods that worked fairly well. Then one day I had a brilliant idea and looked up 'threads' in *Machinery's Handbook* (Oberg and Jones). There have been a lot more threads made in metal than in wood over the years. I should have looked there long ago. Anyway, from the information I gleaned I came up with the plan shown in Fig 3.2 for preparing the two pieces for threading.

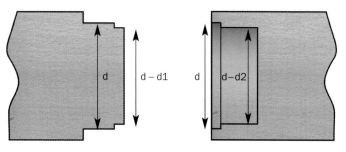

configuration of male and female pieces

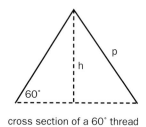

cross section of a 60° thread

Fig 3.2 Finding the dimensions for preparing the male and female parts for threading

$h = 0.866 \times p$

$p = \frac{1}{t_{pi}}$

height of thread $= (0.8 \times h) = 0.69 \times p$

root diameter of thread $= d - (2 \times 0.69) \times p = (d - 1.38 \times p)$

$d1 = 1.38 \times p$

$d2 = (1.38 \times p) + (\text{allowance for clearance, around } 0.020\text{in})$

Basically, it works like this; determine the external diameter you want for your tenon (the male thread, which we'll call *d*), determine the threads per inch you are cutting, then go to Fig 3.2 for the formula to calculate *d1* and *d2*. Next, referring to Fig 3.2, prepare the male portion as shown. Make a small step on the end of the tenon with a diameter of *d* minus *d1*. This step marks the bottom of the thread to be cut. Simply set your cutter so that it touches this step, make sure your threading jig is parallel to the axis of rotation, and cut the thread. The thread will be the proper depth, with no guessing.

Now, referring to Fig 3.2 again, work up the dimensions for the female (or internal) thread. First, cut a shallow recess that is precisely the dimension of *d*. As you will recall from above, *d* is the external diameter of the male thread. This will be the

Fig 3.3 The SG-400 Thread Cutting Jig, sold by Craft Supplies Ltd, is the simplest of the threading jigs on the market

bottom of the internal thread. Cut your threaded section to a slightly smaller diameter, *d* minus *d2*. This gives you the section that, when threaded, will have the proper depth of thread for the internal section. Again, set your cutter to *just touch* the surface of the small recess (with a diameter equal to *d*) and cut the thread. If you measured everything correctly, the two pieces should screw together perfectly. Those metalworking guys know what they are doing.

SG-400 Thread Cutting Jig

There were no instructions included with this jig, however, an e-mail to the supplier, Craft Supplies Ltd, led to a prompt reply. Fortunately, it is not a complicated piece of equipment and I was able to use it without the instructions, though they did have some useful tips that made it easier to use.

Since this jig mounts in the toolrest socket, it can be adapted to work with virtually any lathe. The stem that fits into the toolrest is threaded so that different sized stems may be installed. For example, I bought it with the ½in stem to fit the Carba-Tec lathe. Since I also own stems for 1 and ¾in tool post sockets, I can use the jig on my Carba-Tec, my Record Mini Lathe with its ¾in toolrest socket, and my Nova 3000 (provided that I use my 1¼in x 8tpi–¾in x 16tpi spindle adapter on the spindle nose in order to accept the cutter). This gives the tool a much greater flexibility.

On the Nova 3000 the tool post extension is not long enough to bring the centre line of the threading jig up to the centre line of the headstock. However, since it is only slightly lower, the jig worked well enough on it, and I corrected the problem by making a longer stem to raise the jig to the proper height.

The SG-400 Thread Cutting Jig consists of several pieces, as shown in Fig 3.3: the thread-cutting body, the chuck adapter, the toolrest stem, the cutter holder and the cutter blade.

Another maple box with 6¾tpi threads cut using the Beall Masterpiece Turner

The thread-cutting body

The thread-cutting body is simply a sturdy frame set up to move a spindle back and forth when the hand crank is rotated. On the right-hand side is the hand crank and on the left is a smooth spindle nose to accept the chuck adapter. I purchased the No. 1 chuck adapter, which is ¾in x 16tpi, to fit the Carba-Tec spindle nose. On top of the thread-cutting body is a grease fitting to keep the mechanism well lubricated. On the bottom side is a threaded hole to accept the tool post stem. As one cranks the handwheel, the threaded spindle moves back and forth, thus moving anything mounted on the left end of the spindle back and forth and rotating it so that a spinning cutter mounted on the headstock spindle can cut a spiral groove in the wood. The thread cut matches the thread per inch of the spindle. On my unit this is 2mm.

The chuck adapter

My chuck adapter has a nose thread of ¾in x 16tpi to fit chucks that will screw onto the spindle nose of a Carba-Tec lathe. (You can get different chuck adapters to fit other lathe spindles, which is the beauty of this jig.) It is simply a threaded section with a shoulder for the chuck to fit up against. On the other side it has a hole precision-machined to fit the spindle nose of the thread-cutting body. A setscrew secures it to the spindle of the thread-cutting body.

The toolrest stem

The toolrest stem is threaded to screw into the bottom of the thread-cutting body. This enables you to use several different stems to adapt the jig to different lathes.

The cutter holder and blade

The cutter holder is threaded on one end to fit onto the spindle nose of your lathe. I ordered the No. 1 cutter holder to fit my Carba-Tec lathe, but other sizes are available. On the other end of the cutter holder is a slot to accept the cutter and a setscrew to hold the cutter securely in place. The cutter is made of HSS and is ground to produce a 60° 'V' cut in the wood. To assist in setting the cutter blade for depth of cut, graduations on the cutter are approximately 2mm apart. I recommend that you sharpen the cutter by honing only on the top of the cutting edge, never on the bevels.

Because of the length of the cutter, the minimum internal diameter is 2½in. The cutter must extend further on the pointed side than on the square side in order to keep the square side from hitting the area to be threaded.

For this reason, I purchased the Morse Taper End Mill Holder with drawbar capability and the 60° double-angle shank-type cutter that fits into it (see Fig 3.4). These should be available from most metal machining equipment suppliers. The cutter cuts a cleaner thread than the fly-type cutter used with Craft Supplies' Thread Cutting Jig, and is only ¾in in diameter, allowing threads to be cut in much smaller holes.

Fig 3.4 The Morse Taper End Mill Holder with drawbar and the 60° double-angle shank-type cutter that fits into it

Cutting threads

Set up the jig as shown in Fig 3.3 and install it in the tool post on the lathe. The chuck adapter should be mounted on the thread-cutting body and the toolrest stem screwed into the bottom of the thread-cutting body. The cutter holder and cutter blade can then be screwed onto the spindle nose of the lathe before you mount the chuck holding the piece to be threaded onto the chuck adapter. With all of this done, you are ready to set the equipment up for cutting the threads.

This is really not a complicated set-up, although it does require quite a bit of 'eyeballing' to get the thread-cutting body parallel to the axis of rotation. The height of the thread-cutting body should be such that the spindle nose of the lathe and the nose of the chuck adapter align: this will allow the cutter to cut along the centre line of the workpiece.

What I found to work best was to align the thread-cutting body with the lathe bed, with the spindle extended enough to clear the cutter with the workpiece when fully retracted. Align the cutter horizontally and move the workpiece until the recess you cut for the bottom of the thread just touches the tip of the cutter. Now, make sure that the thread-cutting body is still parallel to the lathe bed. There are no precision measurements in this operation, it is all 'eyeball' adjustment. Tighten everything down and crank the spindle of the thread-cutting body back until the workpiece clears the cutter.

Turn on the lathe. I ran mine at 2400rpm and it cut fairly well. It sometimes helps if you hold the workpiece, which will dampen any vibration and thus give a cleaner thread, as you crank the thread-cutting body slowly to move the workpiece into the cutter. As you continue to crank it in you will cut a nice spiral thread along the section to be threaded. Be careful not to let the face of the cutter touch the shoulder of your workpiece on the external thread or the bottom of the recess on your internal thread because the cutter will damage the shoulder area. You can alleviate this problem somewhat by cutting a recess at the end of the area being threaded: this will allow the cutter to make a complete thread before it hits the shoulder or the bottom of the recess. The recess should be slightly wider than the distance from the point of the cutter to the end of the cutter holder; ie, almost half the cutter width.

Once you've cut over the full length of the threaded area and into the recess, turn off the lathe and examine your work (see Figs 3.5 and 3.6). If there appears to be a good clean thread of the proper depth, loosen the toolrest and move the workpiece away from the cutter so that you can remove it from the lathe. However, if it does not appear deep enough, rotate the cutter so that it clears the wood and carefully crank the handwheel back to clear the cutter with the workpiece. Adjust the cutter to cut a slightly deeper recess, then repeat the cutting operation and check the threads again.

Fig 3.5 Cutting the external thread with the SG-400 Thread Cutting Jig and ENCO 60° cutter

**Fig 3.6 Cutting
the internal
thread with the
SG-400 Thread
Cutting Jig**

There should be a slight flat on the top of each thread. You don't want a sharp top as this is more prone to chipping. It is much more difficult to adjust for greater depth with some cutters, such as the 60° double-angle cutter which is a solid piece, because you have to move the entire toolrest assembly to reposition for a deeper cut.

Now comes the fun part – getting the mating thread to screw onto the thread that you've just cut. In theory, if the inside of the area for the internal thread is the root diameter of the external thread, a perfect thread should be produced. However, such threads probably wouldn't screw together because of overall friction. Changes in humidity will cause their dimensions to alter slightly and a set of tight-fitting threads can seize and become stuck. Of course, you don't want them too loose either. They should screw together with the slight freedom required to keep them from binding.

Once your threads have been cut, you can turn away the sizing tenon on the external thread and be left with a nice threaded box or nut and bolt or whatever you were making. I recommend keeping the sizing recess on the internal thread, especially on threaded boxes since there will be a short area near the shoulder of the box that has no thread. The unthreaded section of the internal thread can then slip cleanly over the unthreaded area of the external thread.

This method works very well for bolts and threaded boxes. Using the method described, it does not matter which of the two pieces you thread first, and you can prepare the areas to be threaded ahead of time without concern as to fitting problems. However, the manufacturer's instructions for using the jig, given below, say to make the external thread first.

Manufacturer's instructions

Turn the tenon to be threaded and leave the workpiece mounted in the chuck. Mount the jig on the lathe and the cutter on the headstock spindle and mount the chuck onto the chuck adapter on the jig spindle. Wind the thread cutter in and out a few times to ensure that it is free running, then wind it back as far as it will go. Bring your box up to the cutter, but about 5mm (¼in) short of the tenon. Check to make sure that the cutter will be parallel to the tenon over its full length, then set the cutter extension to cut at a depth of 2mm (⅛in). Retract the spindle fully, lock everything down, set the lathe for its top speed, turn on the lathe and then slowly turn the hand crank to cut the thread. (See Fig 3.5.) I recommend supporting the wood with your hand to help stabilize it – this is extremely important on very hard woods. Run the thread cutter down the wood and stop the lathe when the thread is completed.

Inspect the thread and if it is not deep enough, adjust the cutter to get a greater depth of cut before making another pass. It is best to cut the thread in one pass if possible as this will produce a better thread. When you are satisfied with the thread, remove the chuck from the jig and mount it on the lathe spindle. Remove the workpiece from the chuck and mount it to receive the internal thread. Cut a recess 4mm (⁵⁄₃₂in) deep to fit the external dimension of the threaded tenon – a slip fit. This is now the bottom of your internal thread. The area where the thread is to be cut should be 2–2.5mm (¹⁄₁₆–³⁄₃₂in) smaller than the diameter of this 4mm (⁵⁄₃₂in) sizing recess. Finish hollowing the lid and remove the chuck from the headstock spindle.

Remount the jig and cutter and mount the chuck onto the jig spindle. Set up in a similar manner to that for the external thread and set the cutter to *just touch* the wood in the 4mm (⁵⁄₃₂in) sizing recess. Wind back the jig spindle until the box clears the cutter. Turn on the lathe and crank the box lid into the cutter. (See Fig 3.6.) For the first two turns the cutter should not be cutting, but after this it will start to cut your thread to the proper depth. It is designed to cut within 3mm (⅛in) of the bottom of the recess. When the cut is completed, stop the lathe, rotate the cutter so that it doesn't touch the wood, and crank the wood clear of the cutter.

You can loosen the tool post (not the banjo) and rotate the workpiece out to check the fit of the threads. If more wood needs to be removed, loosen the cutter, extend it a small amount and re-cut the threads. Repeat this process until it fits. If everything has been done properly, the two pieces should screw together perfectly. You can now finish turn, sand, and polish the workpiece with the two pieces screwed together.

The Klein Threading Jig

The Klein Threading Jig is a little more precise than the SG-400 Thread Cutting Jig. It was designed to work with the Klein Design Lathe and I've seen Bonnie Klein make a threaded box fairly quickly. She has done enough of them that there is little guesswork on her part in relation to dimensions. Most of the time her lids screw onto the box with no adjustments required. The Klein Threading Jig is available with threaded spindles for 16 and 10tpi. The 16tpi is good for most little threaded boxes. In softer woods, the 10tpi is very useful because the coarser thread will be stronger. (Figures 3.7 and 3.8 show the Klein Jig in operation. Figure 3.9 shows the fit of the two pieces after threading.)

The Klein Threading Jig comes with a video that shows and tells you exactly how to make a threaded box or any other type of threaded item within the size range of the jig and the lathe. Adapters are available to fit the threading jig to the Carba-Tec, the Jet Mini Lathe, and the Vicmarc Mini Lathe.

One very good feature of the Klein Threading Jig is that it keeps the axis of the threaded spindle parallel to the axis of rotation so that you're not having to 'eyeball'

Fig 3.7 The Klein Jig cutting an external thread. Hold the work-piece to dampen any vibration

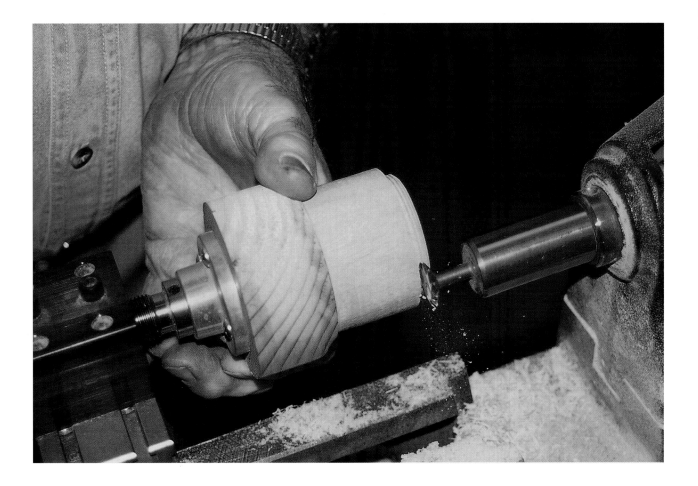

Fig 3.8 The Klein Jig cutting an internal thread. Note the hand crank; this can be used to position the workpiece to get the proper depth of thread

Fig 3.9 The fit of the internal and external threaded pieces cut by the Klein Jig

the alignment. Also, instead of having to adjust the cutter, you move the part of the jig with the threaded spindle on which the workpiece is mounted in and out. There is a precision adjuster that can be used to make small adjustments for depth of thread; to make a major horizontal adjustment you do have to loosen some screws and move the fixture right or left to get it close, but the precision adjuster will then take over. The Klein Threading Jig also uses a different form of cutter. It is a 60° wheel cutter that cuts a bit more uniformly than the single rotating cutter of the SG-400 Jig.

The operation of the Klein Threading Jig is essentially the same as for the SG-400 Jig. You align the workpiece to the cutter, use the precision adjustment to move the workpiece into the cutter, turn the crank on the end of the threaded spindle, and cut a spiral thread on the workpiece that matches whatever threaded spindle you have installed. Inspect the thread and if it appears to be good, remove the workpiece and repeat the process for the mating part. The methods described above also apply to this jig.

The Nova Ornamental Turning Attachment

The Nova Ornamental Turning Attachment, or the Ornamental Turner, is designed to enable people to do decorative ornamental work with a regular lathe. It was designed for use with the Nova 3000 Lathe, but adapters are being designed to fit the unit to other lathes. However, you cannot cut threads with the basic unit. For this you will need to purchase the thread-cutting kit and the side-cutter attachment (see Fig 3.10).

In their manual Teknatool, the manufacturer of Nova products, say to *completely* turn the workpiece that will have the external thread. They caution, as I have done several times, to make sure that the area to be threaded is parallel to the axis of rotation of the lathe. They tell us: 'Do not remove work from chuck before male thread is cut.' The reason for this statement is that you may never be able to get

Fig 3.10 The Nova Ornamental Turner set up to cut external threads. This jig offers more adjustment possibilities than any of the others discussed here

the piece exactly aligned again if you do remove it from the chuck before this. When you have finished, and only then, remove the chuck from the headstock spindle and set it aside.

Installation

To install the Ornamental Turner on the lathe and set it up for threading, follow the steps below.

1. Loosen the collar and then slide it along the spindle to allow the spindle to move freely through the housing.

2. Place the threaded bush on the spindle and fix it in place by tightening the handwheel. The threaded bush is a sleeve with an external thread that the guide

will ride in to cause the spindle to rotate as it is moved forward and back. A 2mm bush is supplied with the basic unit. The 1.5 and 3mm pitch bushes are available in the accessory thread kit.

3 Raise the thread chaser to engage with the threaded bush, making sure that the detent is disengaged from the index plate.

4 Ensure that the axis of the Ornamental Turner is in alignment with the lathe bed, otherwise your threading will taper.

5 Fix the side cutter firmly onto the headstock spindle with the Morse Taper Drawbolt clamping system, if it is a Morse Taper side cutter unit. Check that the cutter is securely installed and facing the correct way to cut. I should note at this point that Teknatool now has a four-bladed cutter available as an optional extra. As this cutter produces the best thread cutting, I recommend that you buy it or one of the double-angle cutters available from ENCO.

6 Set the lathe speed range to about 1800rpm.

7 Secure the chuck on the spindle nose of the Ornamental Turner.

8 Slide the Ornamental Turner towards the headstock until your work is nearly ready to engage with the cutter.

9 Position the loose collar along the spindle and lock it so that it will act as a stop.

10 Set the cross-slide towards the workpiece.

Cutting threads

You are now ready to cut your thread. Move the workpiece towards the headstock horizontally until the tip of the cutter (either the side cutter or the four-bladed cutter) just touches the surface to be threaded. Back the workpiece away from the headstock so that the cutter is now clear of the workpiece. Move the work about 0.5mm (¹⁄₆₄in) towards the cutter. Turn on the lathe and crank the work into the cutter to cut a threaded spiral. Your thread should have a small flat on top. This can be achieved in either one or two passes. (See Fig 3.11.)

Fig 3.11 Cutting the external thread with the Nova Ornamental Turner, using the optional cutter with four blades. The cutter normally provided is a fly-cutter arrangement similar to that used with the SG-400 Thread Cutting Jig

When you are satisfied with the thread, remove the chuck from the lathe and the workpiece from the chuck. Remove the cutter from the headstock spindle and the Ornamental Turner from the lathe and set them aside. Mount the chuck on the headstock spindle and mount the piece to receive the internal thread into the chuck.

Turn the piece to receive the internal thread completely, leaving the internal diameter about 1mm (1⁄32in) smaller than the external diameter of the external thread you have just cut. Remove the chuck from the lathe and set aside. Reinstall the Ornamental Turner on the lathe and repeat steps 4–10 to cut the internal thread. (See Fig 3.12.)

The Teknatool manual states: 'By releasing the holding grub screw on the pedestal base, the Ornamental Turner spindle can be pivoted away to test fit the two pieces. If slightly more needs to be removed, pivot the spindle back to reference with the cutter against the thread. It is important that once threading has commenced, neither the cross-slide nor top-slide handwheels are accidentally altered. If necessary, make the thread deeper in very small increments and retry for fit. The difference between a fit or not can be very small. A loose-fitting thread is not very satisfying. Practise on an experimental piece first to become familiar with the process of threading.'

This feature is not available on either of the other two thread-cutting jigs discussed; you have to destroy your set-up to check the fit on both. Of course, the Ornamental Turner is much more than a thread-cutting jig since you can do a great many ornamental decorations on your turned box as well as make a threaded lid for it.

Fig 3.12 Cutting the internal thread with the Nova Ornamental Turner. In this instance, the operator's left hand is used to dampen vibration

The Beall Masterpiece Turner

Beall Tools, who have made a thread-cutting jig for use with a router, have come out with a device called the Beall Masterpiece Turner (see Fig 3.13). This device has the capability to turn screw threads in wood. The Beall Masterpiece Turner is available to fit the Nova Comet, the Jet Mini and the Carba-Tec, but it shouldn't be difficult to adapt it to almost any lathe that has a spindle extension on the outboard end of the lathe headstock, though it wouldn't work on the Record Power Mini-Lathe, for instance, because there is no outboard extension of the headstock spindle.

In addition to the basic Masterpiece Turner, you'll need a flexible-shaft tool, such as the Foredom or the Dremel, to provide the cutting capability. If you don't have a flexible-shaft tool, I recommend that you buy the complete Masterpiece Kit: it will save money in the end.

Fig 3.13 The Beall Masterpiece Turner mounted on my Nova Comet lathe, set up to cut an internal thread. Of the threading jigs discussed in this chapter, this is the only one in which the workpiece remains mounted on the lathe spindle

This tool allows you to cut threads in a number of pitches. It is very useful for small items such as little threaded and decorated boxes. If you also buy the optional reversing mechanism, it allows you to cut both left-hand and right-hand threads.

Other optional items that may be of use are: the instructional video, which explains what the unit will do and demonstrates how to use it; the Side-Cut Threading Bit; the Masterpiece Stops; and hand taps for ¼in x 20tpi and ⅜in x 16tpi.

The Masterpiece Turner mounts in your lathe's toolrest holder and is attached to the lathe's headstock spindle through a timing belt and an indexing plate that attaches to the outboard end of the lathe spindle. These are the two areas that differ between units for different lathes. You must have an indexing plate that will mount onto your lathe's outboard spindle and you must have a tool post that fits into the banjo of your lathe. This is a fairly long piece to be held steady by the toolrest post alone and because of this, Beall came up with a magnetic support that minimizes any flex or vibration in the unit that could cause problems with your threading. I should add that, like the Threading Jig sold by Craft Supplies Ltd, the Masterpiece Turner does require a bit of fiddling to align it properly with the lathe's axis of rotation. I didn't find this very difficult, however, as it is a matter of visually aligning it with the lathe bed.

The Masterpiece Turner differs from the other threading jigs described here in that you can turn the piece mounted on your headstock spindle, then mount the Masterpiece Turner in place of the toolrest and cut threads or other decorations on the turned piece without removing it from the lathe spindle. The unit can be mounted on the lathe quickly, and if you've followed the rules for sizing the area to be threaded and making a little step for setting the cutter, you can be threading in a few minutes. The tool holder slides in and out so that the cutter can be set to the proper depth in a very short time. Turn on the flexible-shaft tool and crank the hand crank on the Masterpiece Turner to cut your threads. After you have programmed the gearbox to cut the threads you want, it is *that* easy (see Figs 3.14 and 3.15). The manual comes with complete instructions for programming the gearbox so I will not go into it here.

Fig 3.14 The Beall Masterpiece Turner is the only jig with a gearbox that can be used to change the threads per inch that are cut. Here, the gearbox is set up to cut 6¼tpi

Fig 3.15 The Beall Masterpiece Turner cutting an internal thread of 6¼tpi

Fig 3.16 The Beall Masterpiece Turner easily cuts a 6¼tpi thread on the external tenon

Two basic gear combinations can be set up: 20tpi and 16tpi. The 20tpi setting can be adjusted to 12.5tpi and 6.25tpi by simply changing the sprocket diameter of the gearbox drive. With the 16tpi gear setting you can also get 10tpi and 5tpi threads by adjusting in the same way. Figures 3.16–3.18 illustrate the thread cutting of both internal and external threads, the fit of the two pieces, and the finished piece.

Again, the Masterpiece Turner is a pretty sophisticated and expensive piece of equipment for cutting threads alone, however, you also get the capability to cut spirals and

Fig 3.17 The mating of the finished pieces

Fig 3.18
The finished
screw-top box

to create indexed fluting. If these features fit into your turning activities, they may well justify the purchase of this unit. Its ornamental capabilities, when combined with those of the Nova Ornamental turner, give you all the ornamental turning capabilities you will need, except those provided by a Rose Engine Cutter.

Home-made jig

Before I had heard of Craft Supplies' Thread Cutting Jig and long before the Nova Ornamental Turner came onto the market, I made up a small jig for use with my 16tpi thread chaser to cut threads on boxes. It worked fairly well, but I found that I could actually hand chase the threads on the lathe faster than I could use this jig to do the job. Also, the jig limited me to 16tpi threads, whereas with hand chasing on the lathe I was limited only to the sizes of the chasers I owned.

This fairly simple jig is shown in Fig 3.19. I made it from a ¾in x 16tpi bolt and nut and a little scrap wood, using a spindle shank to fit into the toolrest socket of my

lathe. I might have used it more had I owned a cutter to put in the headstock; it would then have functioned in a very similar way to the SG-400 Jig. I have tried it with the cutter I now own and it works reasonably well. The loose fit of the bolt in the nut wasn't a problem with the hand-held chaser, but it did produce lower quality threads when used with a cutter mounted on the lathe spindle. I present this only as a basic idea for the do-it-yourself buff.

Fig 3.19 One of my early home-made jigs in use with a cutter mounted in the lathe spindle. I planned to use it with a 16tpi hand-held chaser to cut threads in little boxes, but found it easier to use a lathe and hand-held chaser

Chapter 4

Using a lathe with a hand-held chaser

One old turning technique that has been gaining interest over the last few years is the art of hand chasing threads. I first became interested in this almost forgotten technique when I began reading Bill Jones' column in *Woodturning* magazine. I had never even heard the term before. Thus began my search, in fact almost obsession, to learn more about this technique and how to use it.

I've been making threads in metal with taps and dies for many, many years, but the thought of cutting threads freehand on a lathe intrigued me. The road from hearing about thread chasing to actually chasing a successful thread was not an easy one, but it has made for an interesting journey.

The learning curve

My first port of call was John Jacob Holtzapffel's book, *Hand or Simple Turning*, in which he devotes a section to the tools used for chasing threads and how to use them on hard wood and ivory items. I read the sections on making and using chasers and tried to make my own, an outside chaser, but it didn't work. Finally, I found a source of used chasers, G & M Tools, in England. They sold chasers singly or in pairs. I ordered several pairs and wound up with chasers for 11, 16, 19, and 24tpi. They didn't work either. I decided the problem must be my lathe speed, my lowest being 500rpm. I even tried turning my Carba-Tec lathe by hand to get the speed down to a manageable level. Nothing seemed to work.

Almost at the point of giving up, I re-read Holtzapffel's book. I read that chasers are used to cut threads in hard woods and ivory, but that a different technique is required for cutting threads in soft woods. I hadn't seen this at first, or at least it hadn't registered.

I began to rethink my definition of hard woods. I had been using maple and apple, considering them 'hard'. With some cocobolo to hand, I chucked a piece to my Carba-Tec, turning the lathe by hand. Thinking that a coarser thread would be easier to cut, I tried the 11tpi chaser. I was wrong, but it worked anyway. Elated, I continued my journey with a search for more answers.

My next purchases were a video by Dennis White (*Boxes, Goblets and Screw Threads*), which includes a section on thread chasing, and James Lukin's book, *Turning Lathes*, which also covers thread chasing well. Whenever I had spare time and a piece of suitable hard wood, I cut a few threads. Incidentally, the chaser I'd originally made now worked. My main problem at this point was defining 'hard wood'.

Wanting to share what I had learned, I wrote an article on the subject for *Woodturning*. This appeared in their June 1997 issue and was reprinted in *Useful*

Techniques for Woodturners, one of 'The best from *Woodturning* Magazine' series. It described chasing threads on a Carba-Tec lathe by turning the lathe with your left hand while holding the chaser with your right. It's a technique that works very well and I've cut a lot of threads in this way.

Both Holtzapffel and Lukin used treadle lathes. Before these, turners used spring-pole lathes, so I graduated to a foot-powered lathe, a spring-pole type with a lathe spindle and three full revolutions per downward stroke. Wow. This was even easier than turning the Carba-Tec by hand. I now had both hands free to work the tool and began to feel confident. Enough so that when I agreed to demonstrate my foot-powered lathe at the January 1997 meeting of The Seattle Chapter of the Association of American Woodturners (AAW), I included thread chasing. Since then, I often demonstrate this technique at craft shows and have progressed to the point where I can chase threads up to 16tpi at 500rpm. I will admit, however, that a speed of 100 or 200rpm makes it a great deal easier. Acquiring a variable speed lathe has expanded the range of threads I can chase. For example, my 4½tpi chasers work quite well on maple when the lathe can be slowed down sufficiently.

Speaking of the softer woods, I've also learned that threads cut much better in the softer hard woods, such as maple and oak, if some end grain is included in the threaded section: if the grain runs across the section being threaded so that it contains some end grain and some side grain, the threads are less likely to break out. This is particularly important when cutting internal threads. When you make a nut and bolt, consider making the bolt shank with the grain running along the length of the bolt, and reversing this so that the grain runs across the hole in the nut and the head of the bolt: this will give a greater thread strength.

I'm sure my journey would have been much shorter had I been able to watch Bill Jones or Allan Batty demonstrate the technique, but this chance didn't come about until after I had learned to chase threads on my own.

A threaded boxwood box with an African blackwood finial. The threads were hand chased using a Sorby 16tpi chaser

Necessary tools and materials

First, you need a pair of thread chasers, one for the inside and one for the outside, as shown in Fig 4.1. When it comes to sharpening the chasers, hone or grind the very top only. Bill Jones and Allan Batty both recommend grinding on the top of the chaser but never, ever on the end of the teeth. I sometimes grind the top and sometimes use a diamond hone; both work very well.

Fig 4.1 A pair of hand-held chasers, with the internal chaser on the left and the external chaser on the right. These are used to cut a 4½tpi thread. I chose them to give a better view of the teeth used to cut the threads

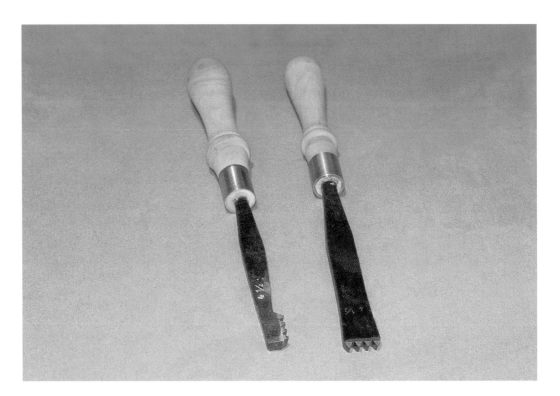

You also need a supply of suitable hard wood. Generally wood that will cut cleanly with a scraper is hard enough for thread chasing. Such woods include lignum vitae, boxwood, Osage orange, desert ironwood, redheart and African blackwood (the best). I've also cut threads in oak, black locust, holly, and mesquite. I've even used a bit of Red Label Hot Stuff CA Glue to render apple wood hard enough for cutting threads, but I don't recommend the softer woods. What you need is a dense, hard wood that will take and hold fine detail. With this defined, let's get to making threads.

Cutting the threads

There was no instruction in anything I read regarding which should be made first, the inside (female) or the outside (male) thread, but Allan Batty recommends making the inside thread first as it is more difficult because you can't see what's going on inside the hole. I agree. Much of my thread chasing practice has involved using a 16tpi chaser to make a thread to fit a ¾in x 16tpi nut. This was always a trial and error situation until I watched Allan Batty demonstrate at Provo in June 1997. He advised making the inside thread first and then, on the end of the external thread, making a short tenon to just fit into the inside thread. This tenon marks the bottom of the external thread, so if you turn till your chaser touches this, your nut or box top should screw on.

The inside thread

Prepare your hole for the internal thread as shown in Fig 4.2. (Refer to Fig 3.2, page 34, to size the areas to be threaded for the internal and external threads.) The only limiting factor for the diameter of the hole is that it must be large enough to enable your chaser to be properly entered. The sides of the hole must be parallel to the axis of rotation unless you want a tapered thread. Lay a straight edge, pencil,

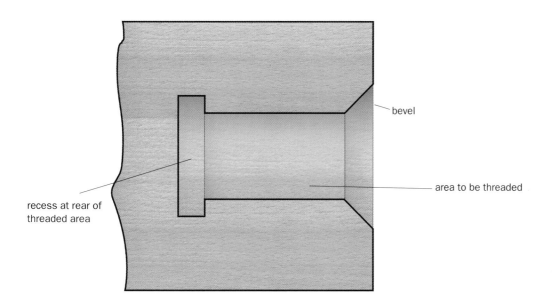

bevel

area to be threaded

recess at rear of
threaded area

Fig 4.2 The configuration of the area for the internal thread. The recess at the rear of the hole allows a complete thread to be cut before the cutter hits the bottom of the hole

or short piece of dowel along the cylinder and compare this with the lathe bed. The entrance to the hole should be bevelled or rounded to prevent the chaser teeth from catching on a sharp edge, and a recess should be cut at the back of the hole to allow the chaser to cut clean before it hits the bottom. When turning the lathe by hand you can feel when you've hit the bottom of the hole; at 500rpm this is not the case. When the chaser cuts into the recess, you must lift the chaser clear and return it to the beginning. Bill Jones refers to this as a sort of figure-of-eight motion. I think of it as a sort of loop.

Holtzapffel says to start cutting your thread on the bevelled part, as shown in Fig 4.3, with your first cuts along the curve a-b and then along the curve c-d, until you are cutting on a line parallel to the cylinder. Lukin says, 'Personally, I have found it quite as easy to begin at once upon the end of the cylindrical part . . .' I agree with Lukin and proceed as shown in Fig 4.4.

I try to have the heel of the chaser ride on the cylinder. It doesn't cut, but it does tend to move the tool along at the necessary rate of speed. A few practice motions like this will help you get a feel for the speed. The more teeth per inch, the easier it is to

Fig 4.3
Holtzapffel's method of striking a thread. I haven't found it necessary to commence the thread on the bevel and prefer to start directly in the recess

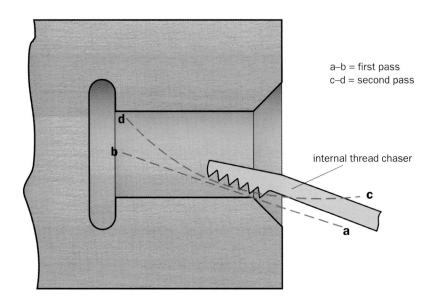

a–b = first pass
c–d = second pass

internal thread chaser

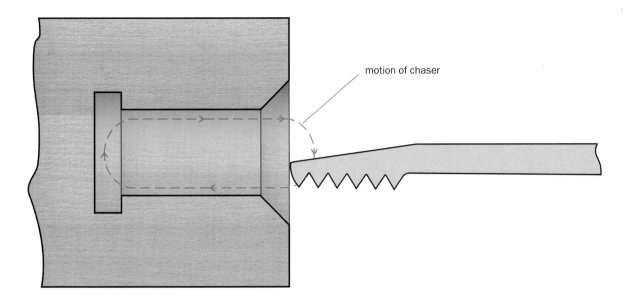

motion of chaser

Fig 4.4 The motion I make with the inside chaser to cut the threads. The chaser should cut clean just into the recess and must be lifted clear before it hits the bottom of the hole

handle the chaser, as the chaser will progress slower; when it moves faster it is difficult to lift clear before the bottom of the hole is encountered. Once you feel you have the speed down, allow it to cut lightly and move it evenly and smoothly, without faltering, at the desired speed. This process is called 'striking the thread'. Once you have grooves cut deep enough to guide the chaser, you no longer have to move it, but you do have to lift it out of the grooves before it reaches the bottom of the hole. You must be careful to insert the tool into the grooves each time; miss and you may cut a double or triple thread, which is not good!

When I began, I turned the toolrest across the face of the area to be threaded, wrapped my fingers around the toolrest and hooked my index finger over the chaser to apply pressure against the cylinder during cutting. Then I acquired an armrest, illustrated in Fig 4.5, which makes cutting the inside thread much easier. To use it, place the handle under your left arm, the armrest on the 'T', and the chaser on the armrest with the turned-up hook touching the chaser. Figure 4.6 shows the armrest in use. It can be tilted up and down as necessary to position the chaser, and pulled back to exert pressure during the cut. Both Bill Jones and Allan Batty consider

Fig 4.5 The armrest, which I find 'indispensable'

turned-up part to rest chaser against

metal part of tool

handle

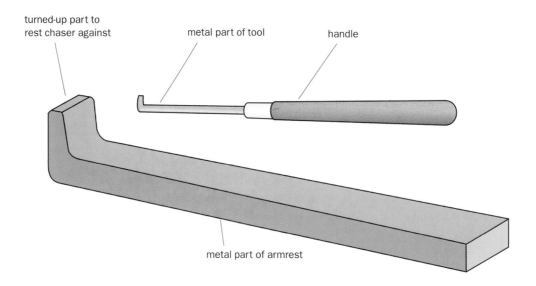

metal part of armrest

Fig 4.6 Pressing the chaser onto the armrest with the index finger while chasing internal threads

the armrest indispensable for internal thread chasing. After using one for several years, I have to agree with them, though I was making internal threads without one for some time.

The armrest is a smooth steel shaft about 7–9in long and ¼in thick. The face is about ½in wide at the handle and less than ¼in at the end where it is turned up at 90˚. The handle will be from 13–15in long with a hole drilled to take a string. The string should be long enough to allow the armrest to hang down your left side, but short enough for you to manipulate to hold the metal end on the toolrest and the handle under your upper arm, pressed against your side. Grasp the toolrest with your left hand and press the tool down onto the armrest and the entire assembly down onto the toolrest with your left thumb. I haven't been able to use my thumb for this process, so I use my left index finger instead. The tool rests against the hook on the armrest so that side pressure can be applied as the threads are cut.

Make additional passes until the thread is deep enough, and clean. If you are trying to achieve a specific size, measure the inside with callipers and, if necessary, shave off a little bit with a side-cutting tool. Make sure the sides remain parallel to the axis of rotation and never remove all of the thread; leave enough to guide the chaser for additional passes, then make more passes until you have a good thread again. I don't hesitate to rotate the lathe by hand and make a few passes with the chaser at this very slow speed as a final touch up. I've also seen Alan Batty do this. If you were to slice the finished piece in half, you should have a thread that appears to be very similar to that shown in Fig 4.7.

Fig 4.7 Cross section of an internal thread

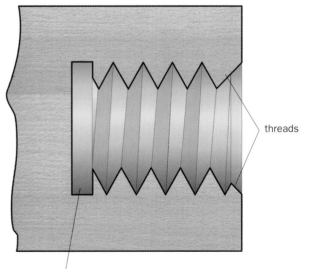

threads

recess at rear of threaded area

The outside thread

Prepare the outside thread area in a similar way to that shown in Fig 4.8. The sides of the cylinder must be parallel to the axis of rotation, there must be a recess cut at the end of the threaded area, a bevel or rounded section at the beginning of the threaded area, and a little tenon (indicated by the shaded area in Fig 4.8) that will

**Fig 4.8
Preparation of
the section
to receive the
external thread**

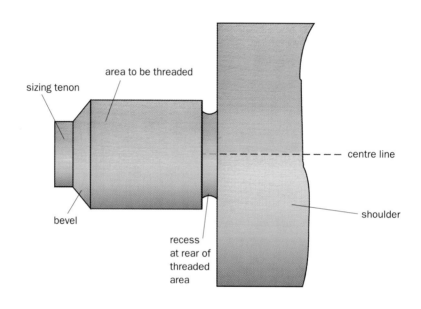

**Fig 4.9 Using the
internal threaded
piece to size the
tenon in order
to establish the
depth of the
external thread**

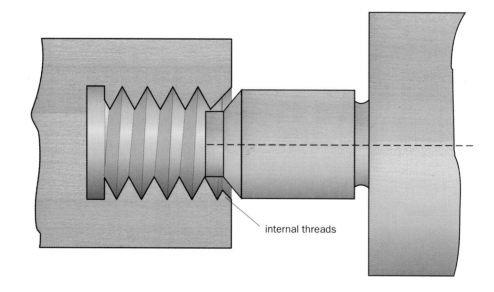

just fit inside the female threaded area (see Fig 4.9). The outside of the cylinder must be larger than this area by at least twice the depth of the threads; ie, if the thread depth is 0.025in then the diameter must be at least 0.050in larger than the tenon. I recommend making it a little larger to allow for mistakes when getting started. This is especially important when first learning the technique.

At this point, I should mention the Thread and Sizing Gauge that was introduced by Robert Sorby in 1999. This tool is somewhat like an inside and outside calliper in that two parts slide back and forth to vary the inside and outside measurements. The difference here is that on the part that measures the outside, one side has a little crosspiece with four arms of different lengths (see Fig 4.10). This crosspiece can be rotated for 10, 16, and 20tpi, or for a slip fit. The tool works well and is very

Fig 4.10 The Robert Sorby Thread and Sizing Gauge. Note the small cross with different length legs – this is rotated into the proper position for the particular threads per inch being used

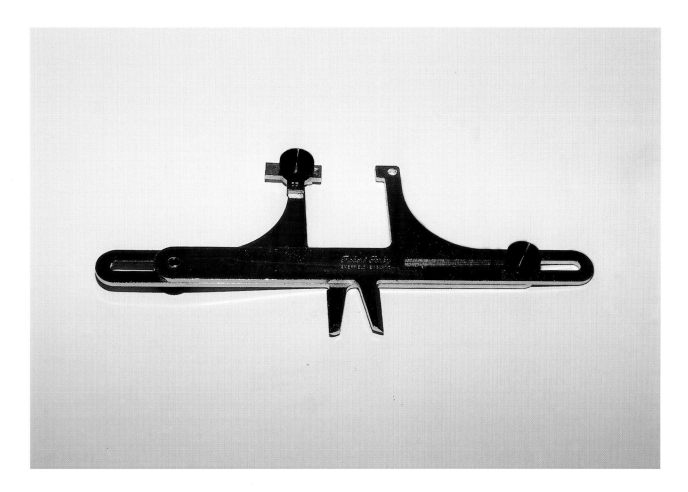

precise – almost too accurate for woodturners just learning to chase threads, as it doesn't allow any material for mistakes. With this tool you chase the internal threads and then measure them with the internal jaws. Set the little crosspiece so that the tpi chaser is facing the other jaw and lock it down with the little knob. This gives you the precise outside diameter of the external threaded area. The tool will work either way, but since the internal thread is the most difficult to do, I feel it is best to do it first.

Before you actually start moving the chaser along the toolrest, it is important that the rest be dressed smooth: any nick or rough spot can stop the chaser or cause it to falter which will create problems with your thread. Again, with the area below the cutting edge rubbing on the wood, get a feel for the necessary rate of feed. Make a

Fig 4.11 The path of the chaser for cutting external threads. When it just marks the sizing tenon, the thread should be ready to receive the internal threaded piece

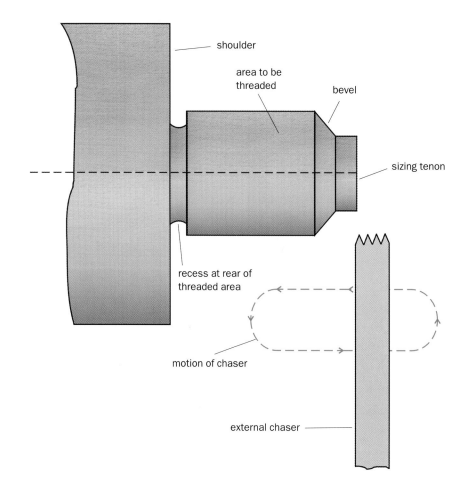

shoulder

area to be threaded

bevel

sizing tenon

recess at rear of threaded area

motion of chaser

external chaser

few trial passes before you allow the tool to start cutting, then move it along evenly at the determined speed, letting the edge cut lightly (see Fig 4.11). Figure 4.12 shows threads being chased on the lathe. As the cutter moves into the recess at the end of the thread area, pull it away from the wood and place it back at the beginning. Your chaser should be moving from right to left. Repeat this operation until the thread is well formed. If the chaser hasn't started to make scratches on the small tenon (indicated by the shaded area in Fig 4.11), use a square-end scraper to make a light cut on top of the threads, then cut them deeper until the chaser just cuts the small tenon.

Fig 4.12 Cutting an external thread on holly using an 8tpi chaser, with the lathe running at about 200rpm

Final adjustments

If you've done everything properly – ensured that the threaded area was parallel to the axis of rotation and cut the threads to the correct depth – the internal thread should screw onto the threads you've just cut, though you may still have to relieve this a bit. I generally turn the lathe off and rotate it by hand while making some final passes with the chaser.

Once you've done this, try your nut or lid again. If it screws on fully but is a little stiff, apply some soft wax and work it a bit. If that still doesn't free it up, take another pass with the chaser while rotating by hand. When everything fits, your thread should look something like the thread shown in Fig 4.13. Figure 4.14 shows the internal and external threads together, with the internal thread cut in half to show the mating of the two.

Fig 4.13 The finished external thread should look something like this. You want a sharp, clean 'V' on the bottom of your threads, but not on the top: here each thread should have a little flat, as it is easy to chip a sharp edge

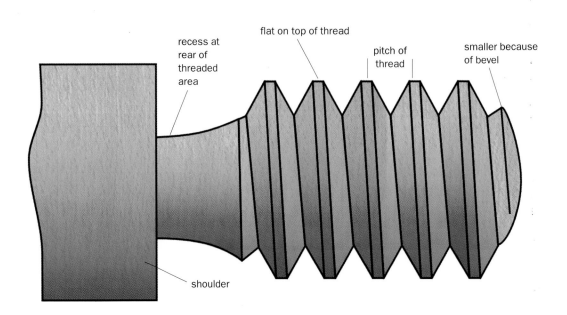

Clean the threads with a soft cloth and apply a light coat of soft wax as a finish. Work the threads a few times to burnish them.

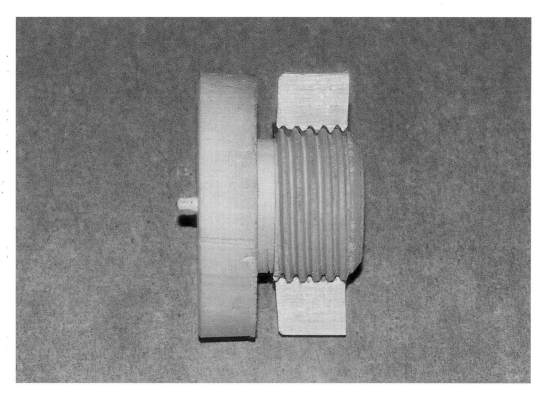

Fig 4.14 Cross section of the internal and external threads together. These are hand-chased 8tpi threads

A final note

Well, that is about all there is to it. As Bill Jones says, '. . . start making little boxes with threaded lids, by the time you've made half a gross, you'll be a thread chaser.' Once you have the inclination, the tools and a little bit of know-how, all you need is a lot of practice. Remember, a lathe with a speed of 100–200rpm is best. Lacking that, try chasing threads while hand-turning the lathe. Start with a fine thread (16–24tpi) and use a good hard wood. One of the best I've used is African blackwood. It is a bit pricey but it sure makes a nice thread. This is one time when you don't want to learn on cheap wood; get good wood so that the learning experience is rewarding.

One final note; all of the discussion here has been for cutting right-hand threads. To cut left-hand threads, move the chaser from left to right. Even though most chasers will be right-hand chasers, you can cut left-hand threads by tilting the chaser down so that only the very cutting edge is contacting the wood. Move at the same speed, but from left to right. Have fun making threads.

PART TWO

Applications

Allan Beecham hand-chasing a thread

Chapter 5

Wooden bolts

I like to make nuts and bolts but I don't normally make items that use them, though there are many construction projects, including furniture designed for disassembly and reassembly, that require the use of wooden bolts. You really can't purchase a wooden bolt in any conventional hardware store, so you will need to make your own for such projects. If the bolt size requirements fit into the standard sizes of tap and screw box, this is by far the easiest way to make a bolt and is the method I recommend. Bolts generally have fairly coarse threads that will hold up well in the softer woods, so you can make them from the same wood used for the rest of the project, although a contrasting wood is often better. The smallest commercial tap and screw box that I've seen is ½in. If you need smaller than this, you will have to resort to the engineers' tap and die set, which generally goes from ½in down to a No. 6 machine screw. For these smaller sizes, you must use very hard, tough wood or the threads will not hold up.

The alternative to using the tap and screw box is to use the hand chaser and the lathe, as described in Chapter 4 (see page 58). The threading jigs described in Chapter 3 can be used effectively on larger bolts, but the size of the cutter is the limiting factor when it comes to making the nuts. The external threads are not a problem, but the cutter must be small enough to enter the hole to cut the internal threads. Most cutters aren't small enough for anything under about ¾in and in the case of the SG-400 Thread Cutting Jig, the cutter is not suited for an internal thread in a hole smaller than 2½in. Hence, for the average project, you will be limited to the use of the tap and screw box or hand chasers on the lathe. Even the hand chasers tend not to work very well for bolts much below ½in in diameter.

Making the bolt

Dimensions

Figure 5.1 shows the basic dimensions for a bolt and nut. The controlling dimension is the diameter of the bolt shaft. The flats on the head should be 1.5 times the

TECHNICAL NOTES

There are two ways to make a bolt. You can make one from oversize stock, turning the bolt shaft down to the desired size while leaving an oversize portion from which to fashion the head, or you can make the shaft and the head out of two different pieces. I have used both methods. With softer woods, such as oak, maple and apple, the two-piece bolt will be stronger. You will need to use the tap and screw box to make these, as soft wood is not hard and dense enough to handle the scraping action of thread chasers. So, if you plan to make your bolt from one of the softer woods, you will be limited to the sizes of tap and screw box available unless you can find a blacksmith to make you a tap and screw box to fit the particular size that you need. For this exercise I chose oak, used a ¾in tap and screw box, and made the bolt 3in long.

Fig 5.1 The three pieces required to make a wooden bolt: the head, which has a recess to hold the bolt shank, the bolt shank, and the nut

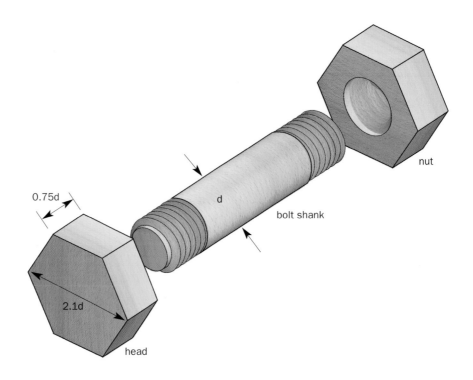

0.75d

d

bolt shank

nut

2.1d

head

diameter of the shaft. On a square head, the dimension across the diagonal from point to point should be about 1.4 times the dimension across the flats, or about 2.1 times the diameter of the shaft. Therefore, to make the bolt from a single piece of wood, the wood must be 2.1 times the final diameter of the bolt shaft. The thickness of the head should be approximately 70–75% of the diameter of the bolt shaft. This means that a 1in bolt should have a head that measures 1.5in across the flats, 2.1in across the diagonal, and have a thickness of about ¾in. The top edges of the square (or hexagonal) section should be bevelled at an angle of about 25–30°. Vary too much from these dimensions, and your bolt will look awkward or ungainly.

If you don't have a lathe and are using a tap and screw box to make your threads, you have little choice but to make your bolt in two pieces. Figure 5.2 gives you a number of concentric hexagonal shapes which can be used as templates for laying

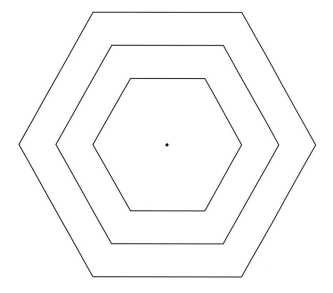

Fig 5.2 Hexagon templates for use in shaping bolt heads and nuts

out the heads of bolts. I should also mention that The Beall Tool Company sells a very neat Hex Nut Template for this purpose. This template also lists tap drill sizes for their various sizes of taps. These sizes seemed to work fine for my taps as well. (Recommended tap drill sizes are given in the table on page 83.)

Select a piece of dowel in the wood you desire for your bolt, checking that it will fit snugly in the input hole of your screw box – not tight, just snug. Cut this to the desired length plus a little extra to allow for the shaft screwing into the bolt head. This extra amount should be less than the depth of the bolt head.

For this bolt, I cut a length of dowel 3½in long for the shaft. Following the basic dimensions given above, the bolt head had to be slightly thicker than ½in and have a diagonal dimension of slightly over 1½in. If you wish to have the wood grain in the head running in the same direction as in the bolt shaft, you will need a piece of wood 1½in sq from which to slice a ½in piece. Using the appropriate template, draw your hexagonal shape on this and mark the centre. Saw or sand back the wood to the layout lines to form the hexagonal shape.

Drilling

Using a Forstner-type drill, make a ¾in hole all the way through this bolt head. This is most easily done if you have a drill press. If you don't, be sure to clamp the piece firmly when you're drilling. Glue the dowel into this hole and leave to dry.

If you have a lathe, it would be fairly easy to turn the bevel on the top of the bolt head. If you don't, I recommend the use of a disc sander, if you have one. Otherwise a hand rasp and sandpaper can be used.

Should you choose to make the bolt head with the grain running perpendicular to that in the bolt shaft, I recommend that you don't drill all of the way through the head, but as deep as possible before the tip of your drill penetrates the top. This will give a more pleasing appearance to the finished bolt than having contrasting end grain and side grain on the top. If you simply glue the shaft of the bolt into the head, I recommend that you also pin it for additional strength.

Cutting the threads

Once the glue has set, clamp the head of your bolt in the vice, placing jaw protectors or blocks of wood on each side to avoid marking the wood. Using the screw box, cut about 1½in of threads on the end of the bolt shaft (see Fig 5.3). If you have some method of bevelling the end of the shaft, do so. This will make it easier for the screw box to start making a thread and will also make the end of the bolt look better. Apply a coat of wax to the entire bolt and buff it with a cloth. This will help to protect the wood and to highlight the grain. It will also make the threads of the bolt and nut work more smoothly as the waxed surfaces will slide together better.

Making the nut

The nut is made in a very similar fashion to the head of the bolt, but with the hole of the appropriate tap drill size – in this case ⅝in. The external dimensions of the nut

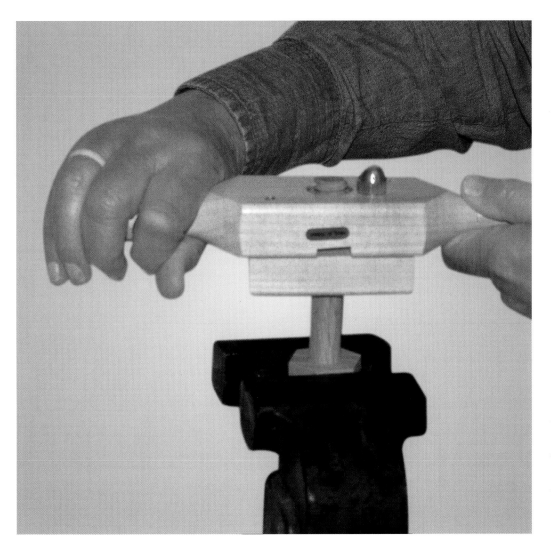

**Fig 5.3 Cutting
threads on the
bolt shank after
the shank has
been secured in
the head of the
bolt; the head is
held in the vice**

should be exactly the same as those for the head. The nut should be slightly over ½in
thick, about 1⅛in across the flats and about 1½in across the diagonal of the square
section. Cut off a ½in slice from a piece of oak that is 1½in sq, lay your hexagonal
template on this, mark the centre and drill a ⅝in hole all of the way through.
Again, I recommend a Forstner-type drill for this, but others can be used if they do
not drill oversize.

Clamp the nut in the vice, using jaw protectors or blocks of wood to keep it from
being marked, and cut the threads with the tap (see Fig 5.4). Make sure the large part

Fig 5.4 As the hole goes right through the nut, only one tap is needed to cut threads. However, it is important to ensure that a full-size thread is cut the whole way

of the tap cuts all the way through the nut. At this point I recommend flooding the surface of the threads with thin CA glue to strengthen them. Once the glue has set – this generally takes a couple of minutes – turn the tap through again to clean off any excess glue.

The nut should be bevelled to about 30° on both sides. As for the head, this would be easier done with a lathe, but a disc sander or rasp and sandpaper will do a fairly decent job. When you are satisfied with the surface of the nut, coat it with wax and buff it with a cloth.

The threads in the nut will be stronger if they contain some end grain and some side grain instead of all side grain. The determining factor here is what sort of stress will be applied to the threads; will you need the extra strength? If you do make the nut from plank material (ie, timber containing both end and side grain), I suggest that you also make the head from plank material, for appearance's sake if for no other reason.

Screw the nut onto the bolt and admire your work.

Fig 5.5 The finished bolt. These can be useful in furniture or in any piece where you would like to avoid metal hardware showing

Recommended tap drill sizes

Tap size (in)	Drill size (in)
⅜	¼
½	⅜
⅝	½
¾	⅝
1	⅞
1¼	1⅛
1½	1⅜

Chapter 6

Threaded spindles

It is not uncommon to have threaded parts in furniture, especially furniture that has been designed to be dismantled and stored in its separate parts for moving. Because such parts can become broken or lost, I feel this is a subject that must be covered.

In such cases we are dealing with an unknown; you have a threaded hole and must make a new thread to fit that hole. You may be lucky and have a tap and a screw box of the right size so that you can make the new screw thread using the screw box, without any problems. But what if you don't have a tap and screw box that match? This may well be the case with old furniture, and this is the situation that we will tackle here.

Rounders

For those who don't have a lathe, a rounder is one of the best ways to make the wood round for cutting the screw. I searched through all my catalogues trying to find a source for these ancient tools with no luck. Hence, I've included instructions for making a rounder to prepare your wood for the screw box. Figure 6.1 illustrates a rounder and how it should be made.

I've seen rounders in different configurations. The one illustrated in Fig 6.1 is simply a block of wood with the corners rounded and long enough to make handles. A tapered hole has been drilled through the centre and a piece cut away so that a cutter can contact the wood and any shavings can fall free. Rounders may have one handle or two. Two handles make them easier to hold

Fig 6.1
The rounder – a simple device that serves to plane a piece of wood to a specific diameter. The device has a tapered hole through which the wood is fed, a cutter to shear the wood to diameter, and an exit hole the size of the finished dowel

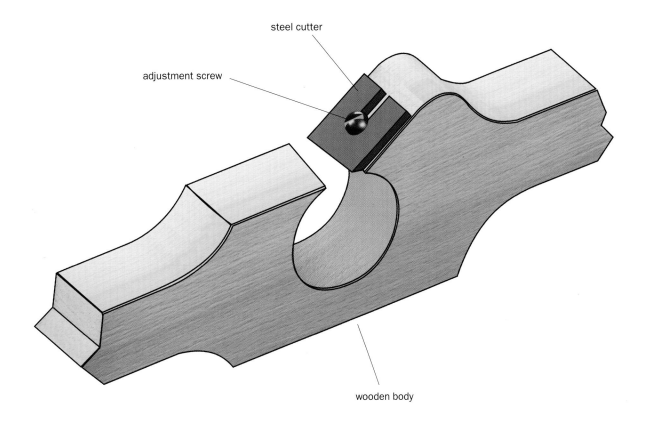

steel cutter

adjustment screw

wooden body

and give more leverage. Handles are most important on larger rounders. I recall reading about a chair factory that used a rounder to make the spindles for their chairs. They mounted the spindle in the lathe between centres, then passed the rounder along the spindle bringing it immediately to size and roundness. It would be mandatory that such a rounder have two handles for maximum stability and ease of use.

You will need to round the spindle roughly before it can be run into the rounder. A spokeshave is a good tool for this preparatory work. Press down on the rounder as it cuts to move it along the spindle.

TECHNICAL NOTES

The first thing to do is measure the threaded hole that you are making the threaded spindle for. You need to measure its inside diameter accurately (see Fig 6.2). This will give you the root diameter of the thread you need on your spindle. You also need to determine the pitch of the thread, ie, the distance from the centre of one thread to the centre of the next. The best way to do this is to use a thread gauge to find the threads per inch of the existing thread. (Or you can simply measure the distance between thread peaks with a small scale, as shown in Fig 6.3.) If you don't have a thread gauge, use a steel scale that will enter the hole and measure as accurately as possible the distance between any two threads.

With these two dimensions, inside diameter and pitch, you can determine, fairly accurately, what the external dimension of the threaded part should be. If you don't have a thread gauge, convert the pitch to threads per inch by dividing the number one by the pitch measurement. Now go to Fig 3.2 and calculate the value of $d2$. Add $d2$ to the inside diameter measurement to obtain the external dimension, or diameter, of your threaded tenon before any threading.

Fig 6.2
Using a calliper
to measure the
inside diameter
of an existing
threaded section.
These digital
callipers provide
great accuracy

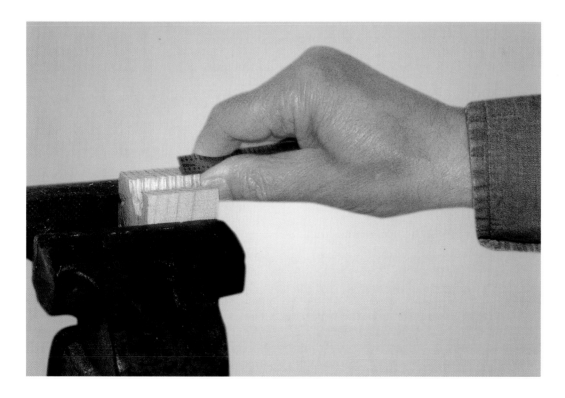

Fig 6.3
Measuring the
pitch of the
thread in the
hole, shown in
cross section

Making a threaded spindle

Turning the tenon

At this point you will need a lathe to turn your spindle to the correct dimensions and to simplify the cutting of the thread by hand, or you will need to make a rounder as illustrated in Fig 6.1 and described above. For the moment I'll assume that you have a lathe.

Turn a short section of the tenon to the exact diameter of the inside of the threaded hole and the rest of the tenon to the calculated dimension. If the piece to be made has a shoulder at the back of the thread, I recommend that you cut a recess next to the shoulder that will match the diameter of the small step on the end of the tenon. This provides a place for the thread to end and will allow the spindle to screw up tight to the furniture piece.

Laying out the thread

There are a number of ways in which to lay out the thread on the spindle tenon. The easiest is probably to cut a strip of paper or tape that is exactly the width of your thread from peak to peak; ie the pitch. (I used the lathe to cut into a roll of masking tape to give me tape that was exactly the pitch of my thread.)

Make one horizontal reference mark on the tenon using the toolrest as a guide. Starting at the right-hand end of the area to be threaded, mark out spaces equal to the pitch along the length of the tenon. If you have a thread gauge, use it to space these marks along the horizontal line.

Now, starting at the left-hand side of the tenon, position the strip of tape or paper so that its right edge intersects the horizontal line and the first thread spacing mark. Anchor the tape in some way (a pin should work well, but I found that the masking tape stuck to the wood sufficiently and no anchor pin was needed), and roll the

This Osage orange box was made from two pieces of plank-wise stock and threaded with 2mm thread, using the Nova Ornamental Turner

Fig 6.4 Winding tape around the section to be threaded. The tape has been cut to the width of the thread pitch

lathe backward while you wind the tape around the tenon. At the next intersection of the horizontal line, the tape should just touch the next thread spacing mark. If it does not, unwind it and change the angle slightly.

Once you have the angle correct and the tape moves around the work to intercept the second thread-spacing mark, you can continue wrapping it around the tenon until you run off the end (see Fig 6.4).

Next, starting with the point at which the right-hand edge of the tape runs off the tenon, mark on the spiral path for the tenon. Do this by tracing along the edge of the tape as you unwind it, to create a spiral as shown in Fig 6.5. You are now ready to cut your thread.

Cutting the thread

Use a 'V' carving tool to cut the thread. It is best if the thread is cut in a single pass, but this isn't always possible. You can use a triangle file to clean up and smooth your chisel work. The chisel cut should be made between the lines that you have laid out on your tenon. When you have finished, the lay-out lines should still be visible, barely, and the depth of cut should equal the depth step that you made on the tenon's end.

It is best to cut the thread in the lathe, as you can rotate the lathe by hand as you cut. This makes it easier to cut along the desired path. If you are having problems, you can also mark this path with a saw to help guide the chisel cut. The saw mark should be close to the desired depth of the thread so that the chisel is effectively

Fig 6.5 As you unwind the tape from the spindle, use a pencil to mark a line along the section still remaining. This will describe the pitch of the thread

cutting on the sides of the thread and not having to cut all the way to the bottom. If you own a power chisel, you may find it makes cutting this groove much easier. Figure 6.6 shows the thread being cut using a power chisel with a 'V' cutter. I feel that I have better control with my power chisel and used it to prepare the work shown in this chapter.

Fig 6.6 Using a power chisel with a 'V' cutter to cut a groove between the lines. When the groove is cut deep enough the line should still remain on top of a small flat

Fig 6.7 The finished thread. If the chisel cuts are not smooth enough, you can use a 60° three-cornered file to smooth the thread

With the thread completely cut, it is time to try it in the hole you are trying to match. If the fit is too tight, try smoothing the thread with a triangle file. Finally, try a little wax on the thread. This often does the trick. Incidentally, my threaded spindle did screw into the threaded hole, after being cut as described here. (See Fig 6.8.)

If you are screwing up against a shoulder, you want the thread to screw in snugly and the shoulder to sit fully against the piece that it is screwing into. It is important that this shoulder fit well because it is the main area of strength. The threads serve to pull the shoulder down firmly.

The procedure described here can also be used to cut threads effectively when you have a tap and no thread box. However, I consider it to be an alternative, to be used only when there is no other choice.

Fig 6.8 The thread fitted nicely into the piece for which it was made

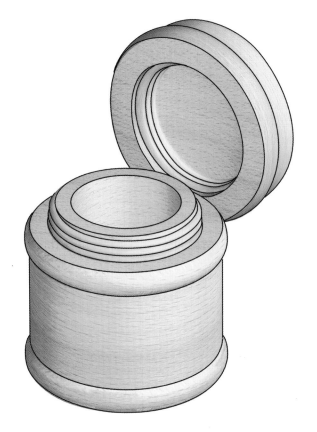

Chapter 7

Screw-top boxes

Australian turner Richard Raffan did an excellent job of covering the small, turned wooden box in his video and book of the same name, *Turning Boxes with Richard Raffan*. He covered overall design and fitting the lid in great detail. He even covered making threaded boxes on a Klein Lathe with the Klein Threading Jig. British turner Ray Key, who is well known for his little turned boxes, has made three videos on box making and design. I'm not going to discuss box design as Richard Raffan and Ray Key have done that much better than I ever could. What I am going to talk about is making the threads on a screw-top box.

Threading methods

On woods that are hard and dense (such as boxwood, African blackwood and lignum vitae), my preferred method is to use the thread chaser. Once you have learned to use this tool, you can thread a box in the time it takes to set up one of the threading jigs. The cost of a set of chasers is much less than that of even the least expensive thread-cutting jig. On softer woods such as maple, apple wood and cherry, however, you'll find the hand-held thread chaser totally unsatisfactory: it is a scraping tool and scraping tools do not cut cleanly on softer woods. The tool of choice for these is the thread-cutting jig. Keep this in mind and you'll soon be making little boxes with threaded lids.

Neither of these threading methods can cut threads all the way to the shoulder on external threads or all the way to the bottom on internal threads. With the thread chaser, you must remove the chaser from the grooves that it is cutting before you reach the shoulder or the bottom of the recess, or you will convert your threads to a number of rings. To allow the completion of a thread, you must use a recess. Allow the chaser to cut into the recess, then lift it before it hits the shoulder. You will have a nice clean thread, plus a recess into which the matching thread can move without friction.

The recess for the external threads can be cut easily with a parting tool but the recess for the internal threads must be cut with an 'L' shaped tool designed for that purpose. Both Crown Tools and Robert Sorby make 'L' shaped tools for cutting recesses. The Crown tool is small and narrow to fit the thread chasers they manufacture. Robert Sorby make their recess-cutting tool with a wider cut for coarser threads, indicating that the user can modify it to fit their needs. You can always grind a little off, but it is difficult to make the cutter wider again once it has been ground. A wider groove gives the beginner more time to lift the chaser before it hits the bottom of the recess.

None of the texts I've read on using a threading jig and rotating cutter has recommended using a recess at the end of the threaded area. I suppose the reason for this is that you don't have to worry about ruining your thread if your cutter does

hit the bottom on your internal thread or the shoulder on your external thread. However, because of the cutter's shape, there is no way you can cut threads all the way to the end of the tenon or the bottom of the internal recess. A 60° 'V' simply will not allow you to go all of the way to the shoulder before the end of the cutter contacts it. Because of this, I recommend that you do use a recess, both at the end of the thread next to the shoulder and at the bottom of the internal threaded area. This recess will provide a friction-free area for the matching thread to move into as the box lid is screwed on tightly.

Grain orientation

With the above in mind, let's talk about the grain orientation in the wood for your threaded boxes. In very hard, dense woods this is not really an important consideration. However, as the wood becomes less tough, the threads tend to break out when the grain runs from the bottom to the top of the box, ie parallel to the axis of rotation on the lathe. This is especially true for the internal threads; you may get a fairly good external thread but run into problems here.

The solution for the softer hardwoods is to orient the grain so that it runs across the box, ie perpendicular to the axis of rotation or what is normally called faceplate or plank mode. When the thread contains some side grain and some end grain it seems to be much stronger and the threads seem less likely to fracture. African blackwood is so hard and dense it is almost like working with metal, so the orientation of the grain isn't an important factor. Maple, on the other hand, will hardly hold a thread when the grain is parallel to the axis of rotation of the lathe. To overcome this, rotate the axis of the wood 90° so that the thread contains some side grain and some end grain and the thread stands up pretty well. On maple I like to cut the thread, flood it with thin CA glue, allow this to set fully, then re-cut the thread to clean up any blobs of glue. Threads that are made in this way stand up much better.

This spalted birch box is not threaded – it has a pop-top lid.
The fit was executed using the Robert Sorby Thread and Sizing Gauge

If you are using hand-held chasers to cut your threads and you want to use the softer hard woods, you will have to use threads with a greater pitch, ie a fairly coarse thread, and leave a larger flat on the top of the thread. I have chased fairly decent threads in maple using an 8tpi chaser, getting the best results when the grain was perpendicular to the axis of rotation so that the threads contained some side and some end grain. I've also cut some very good 2mm threads with this grain orientation, using the threading jig on maple. I often use the 8tpi chaser to cut internal threads in plank-grain oak to make adapters to screw onto my Nova 3000 lathe spindle. Oak makes very nice threads in this orientation.

Accessories

Incidentally, the cutter that I used for this project was not the one that came with the threading jig. I purchased a Morse Taper End Mill Holder and a 60° double-angle shank-type cutter from ENCO, a metalworking supply house. The cutter that came with the jig was essentially a fly-cutter that did not cut as cleanly as this double-angle cutter. The End Mill Holder is threaded so that a long, threaded rod can be used to secure the holder in the Morse Taper. The cutter is held in the holder with a setscrew. When setting up, you have to make sure that one of the cutter's teeth is touching the wood.

TECHNICAL NOTES

For this box I used plank maple, selecting a cube of approximately 2¾in, and a threading jig: the harder woods are scarce and expensive, and most people will find it more comfortable to use a threading jig than hand-held chasers when they begin. With a lathe having a minimum speed of 500–700rpm, the use of chasers is extremely difficult if not impossible. Speeds of around 200rpm are desirable for thread chasing, although you can generally chase threads of around 20tpi on a lathe with a minimum speed of 500rpm.

Making a screw-top box

One final point before we go into production on our box – the lid should screw on tightly with just 1½–2 turns. On fine-threaded boxes I have tended to make too many threads with the result that it takes several revolutions of the lid to remove it. In any case, you want only enough threads for the lid to screw on and be held firmly: any more than that is too much work for the user.

Marking out

Mark the centre of the plank-grain sides with a cross, by drawing diagonal lines between opposite corners, then mark the centre with an awl to aid in aligning the lathe centres. Mount the wood on the lathe and turn the piece to make it round, with no flat areas remaining.

Box making is easiest with a four-jaw scroll chuck and, for this discussion, I have assumed that you have one. The next step is to mark the point of separation for the lid and body of the box (see Fig 7.1). To do this, turn a tenon on each end of the maple

Fig 7.1 The box blank after being turned round, with a tenon turned on each end and the separation between the lid and body marked

'round' to fit the four-jaw scroll chuck with 50mm (2in) jaws. Mark a point about one-third of the length from the tailstock and make a parting cut there, continuing this until only ⅜in of the diameter remains unmarked. Remove the piece from the lathe and separate the lid from the body by applying pressure to one edge, parallel to the grain.

Turning the lid

Fig 7.2 Hollowing the lid to prepare it for threading

The next step is to mount the part for the lid (the short piece) in the four-jaw scroll chuck, turn the face of the piece flat, then hollow the lid to the required depth (see Fig 7.2), making sure that the sides of the recess are parallel to the lathe bed by sighting along a scale held against the side wall.

Now measure the inside diameter of the recess (see Fig 7.3) and, using the information provided in Fig 3.2 (see page 34), calculate the outside diameter of the external thread. On my piece, this happened to be the diameter at the bottom of the internal thread. Set this dimension on the callipers and turn a small recess about 1/16in deep at this diameter. You will use this little step later to set up the position of the threading jig for cutting the threads. Write down this dimension: you will soon need it to size the tenon for the external threads on the box bottom.

Mount the threading jig in the tool-post hole and raise it to align with the centre line of the lathe spindle. Transfer the chuck from the lathe spindle to the spindle of the

Fig 7.3 Measuring the inside diameter of the lid to determine the diameter of the step required

threading jig and position the jig so that the cutter just touches the stepped recess, which indicates the thread depth, and the jig is aligned with the bed of the lathe. This takes a bit of jockeying and eyeballing, but it is pretty easy to check alignment with the lathe bed by sighting over the top of the jig. Once everything is aligned, the jig is parallel to the lathe bed, the cutter is just touching the stepped recess on the lid, and you have enough threads to back off the jig to clear the lid from the cutter, you are ready to cut threads.

Cutting the threads

Fig 7.4 Cutting the internal thread in the lid using the SG-400 Thread Cutting Jig and the cutter from ENCO

Make sure the cutter is not touching the wood before you turn on the lathe. I use a lathe speed of 1500–1800rpm for cutting threads with this cutter. Turn the handwheel on the thread-cutting jig and slowly feed the wood into the cutter (see Fig 7.4). I like to place my left hand on the chuck to help dampen any vibration that might occur from the cutting. Crank the wood in until the cutter is about to hit the

bottom of the recess, turn the lathe off, rotate the cutter until a gap is aligned with the wood, then reverse the cranking process to clear the wood from the cutter. If everything goes well you should have a good clean thread in the top of your box. If the little terminating recess at the bottom of the lid's recess was wide enough, the cutter should have just cut into it before hitting the top of the box, had the cutting continued.

Turning the bottom

Set the box top aside for now, remount the chuck on the lathe spindle and mount the box bottom in the chuck. True up the face of the box bottom and partially hollow it (see Fig 7.5). Be sure not to make the walls too thin before you have sized the tenon for the threads. Turn the tenon down to the dimension that you noted earlier. Referring to Fig 3.2 (see page 34), determine the diameter for the bottom of the threads and turn a short tenon to that size on the end of the area to be threaded.

Fig 7.5 Hollowing the main part of the box prior to cutting the threads on the tenon; if the hollowing is done after the threads are cut, they may no longer fit

You can also base the size of this tenon on the threads in the lid, making the tenon so that the lid has a slip fit over it. This little step tenon will be what you set the cutter of the thread-cutting jig against.

Cut a recess at the rear of the area to be threaded, against the shoulder of the box. The actual width of this recess is the distance from the end of the cutter to the point of the 'V', which will vary depending upon the cutter being used. This is as close as you can get to the shoulder without damaging it. Turn a slight bevel on the beginning edge of the area to be threaded.

Cutting the threads

Remove the chuck from the lathe spindle and mount it on the threading jig. Mount the cutter in or onto the lathe spindle. Now, position the threading jig so that a tooth of the cutter is just touching the step on the end of the threaded area. This sets the depth of cut or the diameter of the bottom of the thread. Make sure the cutter is clear of the wood then turn on the lathe. Turn the hand crank and cut the thread until the cutter is just shy of the shoulder or until the thread has cut into the recess at the back of the area to be threaded (see Fig 7.6).

If all your measurements and calculations were correct, the lid should screw onto the box bottom. You can loosen the tool post locking screw and rotate the thread-cutting jig to check the fit. With the lid screwed up snug, remove the chuck from the threading jig and remount it on the lathe spindle so that you can finish turn the box as if it were one piece (see Fig 7.7).

Finishing the base

You now have two options for holding the box bottom in order to finish the base: you can mount a piece of scrap wood in the chuck and turn a set of internal threads to match those of the box bottom or you can mount a piece of scrap in the chuck and

Fig 7.6 Cutting the external thread on the box bottom. I support the chuck with my left hand to dampen any vibration

Fig 7.7 With the lid screwed into place the final shape of the box is turned, including any decoration. It is best to do all final sanding and finishing of the outer surfaces at this time

Fig 7.8 Using a jam chuck to hold the box for turning the bottom

turn a tenon to accept the inside of the box. Because the inside of my box walls were parallel I chose, in this case, to use the second option – the jam chuck tenon. The tenon must be a snug fit to the inside of the box and it must have a shoulder for the lip of the box to jam against. This ensures that the box is properly aligned and not canted (see Fig 7.8).

Now, as a minimum, you can turn the bottom of the box to make it flat so that it will not rock when set on a flat surface and to ensure that it is not leaning at an angle, but I always like to put some form of decoration on the bottom so that people looking at it will recognize that I have taken the trouble to finish turn it. I also like to recess the centre of the bottom so that the box is sitting on a rim of about ¼in around the outside diameter. Set the finished box onto a flat surface and admire your work.

Using hand-held chasers

If you don't want to purchase a thread-cutting jig but do wish to spend time learning to use hand-held thread chasers, you can finish little boxes from maple and other softer hardwoods by making threaded inserts for the top and bottom of the box. Use a very hard wood, such as boxwood or African blackwood, to make the threaded inserts, then glue them into your box.

One fellow that I taught to hand-chase threads had been producing stash boxes for a number of years and the thought of making them threaded really appealed to him. He did this very thing, and the contrasting colour of the darker, harder wood at the join made the boxes even more attractive. Mike Mahoney, a production turner in Provo, Utah, makes cremation urns with a threaded lid. The threads are hand chased in a contrasting hardwood. The female thread is a ring that is inset into the body of the urn. The male thread is generally turned on the lid, which is made of the same wood as that used for the inserted ring. This method is very easy, because it is extremely easy to cut an internal thread in a ring with no shoulder or bottom to interfere with your threading.

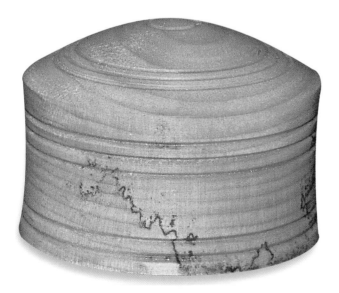

Fig 7.9 The finished box

Chapter 8

Walking stick joins

When I was younger and my wife and I did a lot of camping and hiking in the woods, I always picked up a suitable stick, around 5–6ft (1.5–1.8m) long and 1½in (38mm) in diameter at the largest end, and used it for stability along the trail. It helped to push me uphill when I was climbing and it helped me to put a brake on when I was descending a slope. I generally adopted this stick for the duration of the camping trip if it was a good one, then discarded it when we went home.

Well, we don't go camping anymore and I don't hike on hillsides, but I do still walk along the side of the road and sometimes the uneven ground makes me a bit unsteady. I had thought of making a walking stick for several years. Finally, I selected some square dogwood stock that I had and began work on my first home-made walking stick. I wanted it to be about 5ft (1.5m) long and 1½in (38mm) in diameter at the handhold area, but I also wanted to be able to take it in a motor vehicle should I wish to go hiking in the hills. This meant at least one join to get it down to a good transportable length.

The join

Suitable materials

I didn't think that the brass joins available for canes would be heavy enough for my walking stick. Initially I made up a join from lignum vitae, but it didn't work out because the female portion became too thin to stand up to the pressure and it cracked. It was redesign time! I decided that a ¾in pipe coupling should be about the right size. I made up two male-threaded pieces from lignum vitae, with ¾in tapered pipe threads on one end and a tenon on the other to join to the walking stick. I had an insert from a pipe-threading machine, so I clamped this into a pair of vice grips and used it as a thread chaser. The iron coupling looked ghastly, according to my wife. A visit to the hardware store turned up a brass coupling with a hex exterior shape. She didn't like that either.

I mounted a piece of Osage orange in one of my Nova chucks and chased a thread for the coupling. Using an ⅛in parting tool, I faced off the end of the coupling until it was square with the threads, reversed it so that the faced-off end was against the shoulder on the threaded Osage orange piece, then faced off the other end. Now both ends were square to the threads. Using the ⅛in parting tool, I then turned away the hex shape of the coupling, sanded and polished. It looked great on the walking stick and my wife was happy with it too.

Rather than trying to make the wood of the stick blend in perfectly with the brass coupling to give a seamless join, I turned a bead on either side of the coupling. This created a shoulder for it to butt against at either end, and gave a perfect fit. I turned

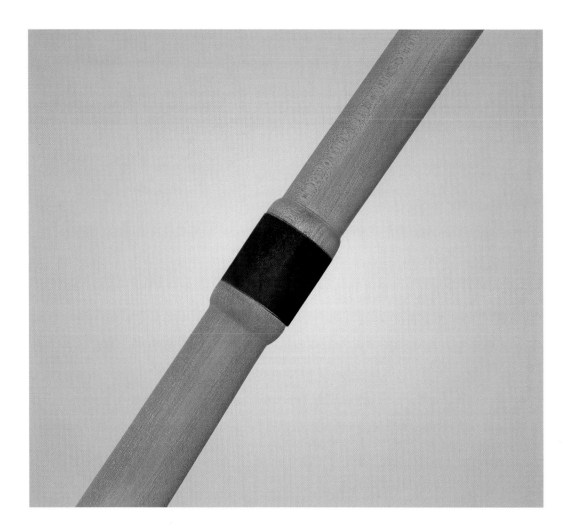

Fig 8.1 The join used on my first walking stick

the wood above and below the beads so that it looked like the wood continued right through the coupling. Figure 8.1 shows the results of this first walking stick join.

I've now made a number of walking sticks for use when taking a normal walk or hike, all around the same length and diameter. Something this long and slender is difficult to turn on a lathe as a single piece. Walking sticks and canes of average height are generally short enough that they don't have to be dismantled to fit in a motor vehicle, however, it is nice if they can be made smaller for ease of transportation and storage even though they seldom exceed 3ft (1m) in length.

For these reasons, I always make them in two or three pieces so that they can be dismantled for transporting and storing.

As mentioned above, when I first started making walking sticks I chose to make the join out of lignum vitae, because it is a very hard and dense wood. It takes threads well and provides a nice contrasting colour at the join. Unfortunately, lignum vitae is very difficult to glue, so I recommend something else for a project of this sort. I have continued to use the brass pipe coupling on all of my walking sticks and that is what I used for this piece.

As I live in the United States, the dimensions given here are American Standard; pipe dimensions will probably vary in other parts of the world. The pipe couplings that I use have a tapered thread and pretty much follow the sizes and shapes shown in Fig 8.2. The coupling I selected for this exercise was a ⅜in pipe coupling made to couple two pieces of pipe with an outside dimension of 0.675in. The threaded

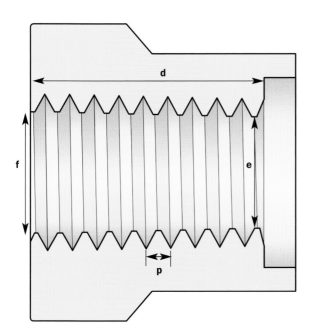

Fig 8.2 The basic configuration of the internal threads on a pipe coupling

f = diameter at entrance
d = length of threaded section
e = diameter at end of internal thread
p = thread pitch (¼tpi)

section needs to be between 0.4 and 0.5in long, with the smallest diameter of the taper around 0.612in and the largest diameter of the taper measuring 0.627in. The thread for this coupling is 18tpi – an easy thread to hand chase.

Strength

When I made my first walking stick, I didn't want the lignum vitae to show, so I let the brass coupling butt against the wood of the walking stick. This is fine as long as the glue joint is secure, but unfortunately it put excessive tension on my glue joint. As a result of this experience, on later sticks I put a shoulder on the lignum vitae for the pipe coupling to butt against. I also found that gluing the tenon into the walking stick body and then drilling and pinning the tenon helped to prevent the glue joint breaking.

TECHNICAL NOTES

For this project I used African blackwood, but any hard dense wood will do. I made ½in tenons that were 1in long to hold the threaded piece into the main section of the walking stick. The shoulder piece must be at least as large in diameter as the basic walking stick body and about ⅛in thick. The threaded section will be at least ½in in length. As a result, the piece of wood for each section must be at least 1 + ⅛ + ½in, ie 1⅝in long.

If you wish to turn them both at the same time, as I did, double this and add enough to handle the width of your parting tool. I added ⅛in for the parting cut, so I needed a piece of African blackwood 3⅜in long and about 1in in diameter.

Making a jointed walking stick

Marking out

Begin by mounting a piece of wood on the lathe, between centres, and turning it round. I like to use a pair of dividers to lay out the various sections on the wood. Set the dividers to ½in to mark a line ½in in from each end; this indicates the threaded sections. Reset the dividers to ⅛in to mark a line ⅛in from the line just scribed on each end; this designates the width of the flange. The section in the centre of the wood should be enough for two 1in tenons plus a ⅛in area for parting the two pieces. If you measure everything correctly, there should be a ⅛in space at the centre for parting off. The laid-out section should look something like that shown in Fig 8.3.

Fig 8.3 African blackwood turned to the correct diameter and marked off for final turning to size. The areas to be threaded are located on each end and the tenon section is located in the centre

Starting to turn

Set a pair of spring callipers to the dimension of the smallest part of the taper on the threaded area. Then, using the callipers and a parting tool, reduce each end to that diameter. Next, set the callipers to the diameter of the largest part of the taper on the threaded area and make a parting cut to that depth next to the outside shoulder on each end. You have now laid out the largest and smallest diameters of the two threaded areas.

Cut a taper from the largest diameter down to the sizing cut on each end and you have your tapered sections turned to size. Now, using the parting tool, cut a recess at the largest diameter, right against the shoulder, for the threading cutter to cut into, and slightly round over the very end of the threaded area to assist in starting the threads (see Fig 8.4).

Fig 8.4 The ends tapered and ready for threading. The threads may be chased at this point while the wood is as stable as possible, before the centre section is reduced to the size of the mounting tenon

Chasing the threads

Set the lathe speed as slow as possible or around 200–300rpm. Now, using an 18tpi external chaser, cut the threads over the tapered section on the tailstock end of the workpiece. Follow the instructions for chasing threads in Chapter 4 (see pages 63–72). Be sure to pull the chaser free from the wood just as it cuts into the recess near the shoulder. When the threads appear to be deep enough you can stop the lathe and try the brass coupling on the wood threads. If everything is sized properly, and the threads are cut deep enough, the coupling should screw on and up snug to the shoulder. If it doesn't, mount the wood again and cut the threads a bit deeper until it does fit. Flip the wood end-to-end, and cut the threads on the other end in the same manner.

Parting off

Set the callipers to ½in and part in next to the shoulder, on the centre side of each shoulder, until the callipers will just slip over the cut. Repeat near the centre of the tenon area, then turn the tenon section down until the three sizing cuts blend in from shoulder to shoulder. At this point your callipers should fit over the tenon along its length (see Fig 8.5).

Fig 8.5 The piece finish turned to size and threaded on each end. Using the Steb-centre in the drive end simplified swapping the ends to chase the threads

Part the two pieces at the centre. You can also cut them apart with a saw if you prefer. The two wooden parts of the walking stick join are now complete. All that remains is to turn the brass pipe coupling to size, true its ends and polish it.

Turning the coupling

Mount a piece of suitable hard wood in a chuck and turn a tenon about ½in long and to the dimensions for the threaded portion of the join. Cut a recess near the shoulder of the piece and thread it at 18tpi, to fit the pipe coupling. Screw on the coupling and true up the end with an ⅛in parting tool (see Fig 8.6). Remove the coupling and reverse it so that the trued shoulder is now against the shoulder on the threaded section of wood. True the other end and then turn the outside to size with the parting tool. I generally bring up the tailstock for support during this operation. Turn to size and polish through the various levels of paper until it has a high shine and the job is done. Screw in each of the threaded pieces and turn the shoulder section to match the brass coupling (see Fig 8.7). Remove the coupling from the lathe and screw in the two end pieces. The walking stick join is completed as shown in Fig 8.8.

Fig 8.6
A threaded section cut to accept the pipe coupling. The end must be faced off to make it true with the threads

Fig 8.7 After the brass coupling has been turned clean and polished, the threaded pieces are screwed into the coupling and the shoulder turned down to fit the coupling

Finishing

At this point I like to drill the two pieces for the walking stick and glue in the tenons of the threaded sections of the join. There is already a centre point in the threaded section. Mount this at the tailstock end, turn the section of the walking stick to final shape, then polish and finish. Repeat for the other section and the walking stick is ready for use.

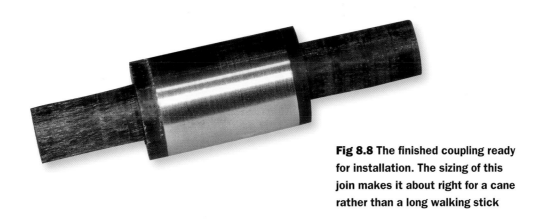

Fig 8.8 The finished coupling ready for installation. The sizing of this join makes it about right for a cane rather than a long walking stick

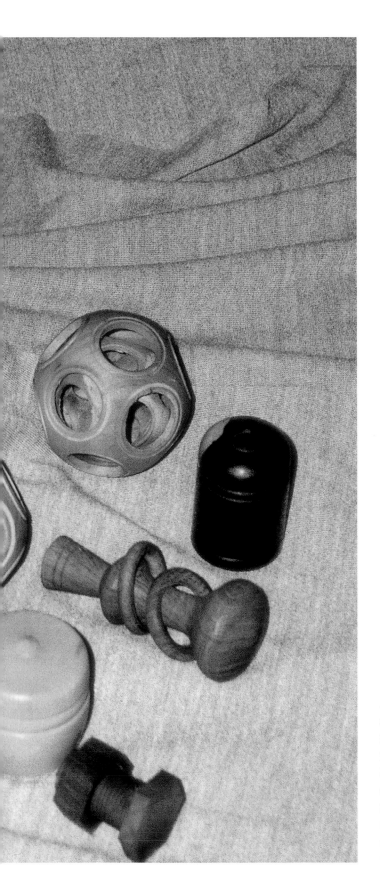

A selection of items turned by the author. Anticlockwise from top: bowl in cherry with textured exterior; mushroom; scoop; miniature goblet; lace bobbins; wine bottle stopper with spiral decoration; wooden bolt with hand-chased threads; threaded box in boxwood; baby rattle with captive rings; threaded box in African blackwood; Chinese balls

Sources

Suppliers of thread chasers

Craft Supplies USA

1287 E 1120 S

Provo, UT 84606, USA

Tel: (800) 551 8876

G & M Tools

The Mill, Mill Lane

Ashington

West Sussex RH20 3BY, UK

Tel: (01903) 892510

Peter Child Woodturning Supplies

The Old Hyde

Little Yeldham, Nr Halstead

Essex CO9 4QT, UK

Tel: (01787) 237291; Fax: (01787) 238522

e-mail: info@peterchild.co.uk; http://www.peterchild.co.uk

The ToolPost

35 Brunstock Beck

Didcot

Oxfordshire OX11 7YG, UK

Tel: (01235) 810658; Fax: (01235) 810905

e-mail: peter@toolpost.co.uk; http://www.toolpost.co.uk

Tracy Tools Ltd

2 Mayors Avenue

Dartmouth

South Devon TQ6 9NF, UK

Tel: (01803) 833134

Woodcraft

210 Wood County Industrial Park

PO Box 1686

Parkersburg, WV 26102–1686, USA

Tel: (800) 225 1153

Manufacturers of thread chasers

Crown Hand Tools Ltd

Excelsior Works

Burnt Tree Lane, Hoyle Street

Sheffield S3 7EX, UK

Tel: (0114) 272 3366; Fax: (0114) 272 5252

e-mail: infor@crowntools.com; http://www.crowntools.com

Robert Sorby

Athol Road

Sheffield S8 0PA, UK

Tel: (0114) 225 0700; Fax: (0114) 225 0710

e-mail: sales@robert-sorby.co.uk; http://www.robert-sorby.co.uk

Jigs for cutting threads

The Beall Tool Company

541 Swans Road NE

Newark, OH 43055, USA

Tel: (800) 331 4718; Fax: (740) 345 5880

e-mail: jrbeall@bealltool.com

Craft Supplies Ltd

The Mill

Millers Dale, Nr. Buxton

Derbyshire SK17 8SN, UK

Tel: (01298) 871636; Fax: (01298) 872263

e-mail: sales@craft-supplies.co.uk; http://www.craft-supplies.co.uk

Klein Design Inc

17910 SE 100th Street

Renton

WA 98059–5323, USA

Tel: (425) 226 5937; Fax: (425) 226 2756

Teknatool International Ltd

PO Box 180034

Luckens Point

Auckland, NZ

Tel: (9) 837 6900; Fax: (9) 837 6901

e-mail: sales@teknatool.com; http://www.teknatool.com

Taps and screw boxes

The Beall Tool Company

541 Swans Road NE

Newark, OH 43055, USA

Tel: (800) 331 4718; Fax: (740) 345 5880

e-mail: jrbeall@bealltool.com

Leichtung Workshops

1108 N Glenn Road

Casper, WY 82601, USA

Tel: (800) 321 6840; Fax: (800) 853 9663

Peter Child Woodturning Supplies

The Old Hyde

Little Yeldham, Nr Halstead

Essex CO9 4QT, UK

Tel: (01787) 237291; Fax: (01787) 238522

e-mail: info@peterchild.co.uk; http://www.peterchild.co.uk

The ToolPost

35 Brunstock Beck

Didcot

Oxfordshire OX11 7YG, UK

Tel: (01235) 810658; Fax: (01235) 810905

e-mail: peter@toolpost.co.uk; http://www.toolpost.co.uk

Trend-Lines

135 American Legion Highway

Revere, MA 02151, USA

Tel: (800) 877 7899; Fax: (800) 735 3825

Rounders

Ashem Crafts

2 Oakleigh Avenue

Hallow

Worcestershire WR2 6NG, UK

Tel: (01905) 640070

e-mail: enquiries@ashemcrafts.com; http://www.ashemcrafts.com

Japan Woodworker Catalog

1731 Clement Avenue

Alameda, CA 94501, USA

Tel: (800) 537 7820

http://www.japanwoodworker.com

Bibliography

Beall, J. R., *The Nuts & Bolts of Woodworking*, J & J Beall Inc, Ohio, USA

Bell, Charles, 'The Gentle Art of Thread Chasing', *Woodturning*, No. 61, pp 56–60, Guild of Master Craftsman Publications Ltd, East Sussex, UK

Holder, Fred, 'Chasing Threads', *American Woodturner*, Vol. 14, No. 2, pp 33–36, American Association of Woodturners, Minnesota, USA

—— 'Thread Chasing Tools: How They're Made', *More Woodturning*, Vol. II, No. 2, p 5, Fred Holder, Washington, USA

—— 'Notes on Hand Chasing Threads', *More Woodturning*, Vol. II, No. 2, p 5, Fred Holder, Washington, USA

—— 'Allan Batty on Thread Chasing', *More Woodturning*, Vol. III, No. 8, p 1, Fred Holder, Washington, USA

—— 'How to Chase Threads in Wood', *More Woodturning*, Vol IV, No. 1, pp 2–4, Fred Holder, Washington, USA

—— 'Questions and Answers from the Internet: Bonnie Klein Threading Jig, Thread Chasing, Making Chasers', *More Woodturning*, Vol IV, No. 1, p 11, Fred Holder, Washington, USA

—— 'Making Threads with Crown Tools', *More Woodturning*, Vol. IV, No. 4, p 7, Fred Holder, Washington, USA

—— 'Getting the Thread', *Woodturning*, No. 53, pp 55–56, Guild of Master Craftsman Publications Ltd, East Sussex, UK

—— 'Uncommon Cutters', *Woodturning*, No. 80, pp 59–60, Guild of Master Craftsman Publications Ltd, East Sussex, UK

Holtzapffel, John Jacob, *Hand or Simple Turning*, originally published 1881 by Holtzapffel & Co, London; published in the UK by Constable and Co Ltd, London and in the US by Dover Publications Inc, New York, USA

Jones, Bill, *Bill Jones' Notes from the Turning Shop*, Guild of Master Craftsman Publications Ltd, East Sussex, UK

—— *Bill Jones' Further Notes from the Turning Shop*, Guild of Master Craftsman Publications Ltd, East Sussex, UK

Klein, Bonnie, 'Turning a Box with a Threaded Lid', *More Woodturning*, Vol. II, No. 2, pp 2–3, Fred Holder, Washington, USA

Lukin, James, 'Cutting Screws in Wood by the Hand Chaser', *More Woodturning*, Vol. II, No. 2, p 6, Fred Holder, Washington, USA (Reprinted from *Turning Lathes, A Guide to Turning, Screw-Cutting, Metal-Spinning, Ornamental Turning, Etc.*, 4th edn (1894))

Mortimer, Stuart, *Techniques of Spiral Work*, pp 159–165, Linden Publishing Inc, California, USA

Oberg, Erik and Jones, F. D., *Machinery's Handbook*, The Industrial Press, New York, USA

Richardson, M. T. (ed.), *Practical Blacksmithing*, Vol. II, originally published 1889–1891 as part of a four-volume set; reprinted as a single volume by Weathervane Books, New York, USA

Starr, Richard, 'Chasing Large Wooden Threads', *Fine Woodworking* magazine, No. 60, pp 53–57, The Taunton Press, Connecticut, USA

Underhill, Roy, *The Woodwright's Work Book*, The University of North Carolina Press, North Carolina, USA and London, UK

Woodruff, Chuck, 'Some Ramblings on Hand-Chased Threads', *More Woodturning*, Vol. II, No. 2, p 6, Fred Holder, Washington, USA

About the author

Fred Holder has been turning wood for over 12 years, experimenting with different techniques and forms including segmented work, multi-centred work, bowls, balls, boxes, and chasing threads. His work is centred on small items, such as lace bobbins, spinning tops, mushrooms, goblets, scoops and bowls.

He has demonstrated woodturning at many fairs and exhibitions in the USA, and passes on his skills through teaching and writing. His articles have appeared in *Woodturning*, *American Woodturner*, *Black Powder Times*, and *More Woodturning*.

Past President of the Northwest Washington Woodturners Chapter of the American Association of Woodturners (AAW), Fred spearheaded the formation of this group in February 1996. He lives on Camano Island, Washington, USA.

Index

TITLES AVAILABLE FROM
GMC Publications

BOOKS

WOODCARVING

The Art of the Woodcarver	*GMC Publications*
Carving Architectural Detail in Wood:	
The Classical Tradition	*Frederick Wilbur*
Carving Birds & Beasts	*GMC Publications*
Carving the Human Figure: Studies in Wood and Stone	*Dick Onians*
Carving Nature: Wildlife Studies in Wood	*Frank Fox-Wilson*
Carving Realistic Birds	*David Tippey*
Decorative Woodcarving	*Jeremy Williams*
Elements of Woodcarving	*Chris Pye*
Essential Woodcarving Techniques	*Dick Onians*
Further Useful Tips for Woodcarvers	*GMC Publications*
Lettercarving in Wood: A Practical Course	*Chris Pye*
Making & Using Working Drawings	
for Realistic Model Animals	*Basil F. Fordham*
Power Tools for Woodcarving	*David Tippey*
Practical Tips for Turners & Carvers	*GMC Publications*
Relief Carving in Wood: A Practical Introduction	*Chris Pye*
Understanding Woodcarving	*GMC Publications*
Understanding Woodcarving in the Round	*GMC Publications*
Useful Techniques for Woodcarvers	*GMC Publications*
Wildfowl Carving – Volume 1	*Jim Pearce*
Wildfowl Carving – Volume 2	*Jim Pearce*
Woodcarving: A Complete Course	*Ron Butterfield*
Woodcarving: A Foundation Course	*Zoë Gertner*
Woodcarving for Beginners	*GMC Publications*
Woodcarving Tools & Equipment Test Reports	*GMC Publications*
Woodcarving Tools, Materials & Equipment	*Chris Pye*

WOODTURNING

Adventures in Woodturning	*David Springett*
Bert Marsh: Woodturner	*Bert Marsh*
Bowl Turning Techniques Masterclass	*Tony Boase*
Colouring Techniques for Woodturners	*Jan Sanders*
Contemporary Turned Wood: New Perspectives	*Ray Leier, Jan Peters &*
in a Rich Tradition	*Kevin Wallace*
The Craftsman Woodturner	*Peter Child*
Decorative Techniques for Woodturners	*Hilary Bowen*
Fun at the Lathe	*R.C. Bell*
Illustrated Woodturning Techniques	*John Hunnex*
Intermediate Woodturning Projects	*GMC Publications*
Keith Rowley's Woodturning Projects	*Keith Rowley*
Practical Tips for Turners & Carvers	*GMC Publications*
Turning Green Wood	*Michael O'Donnell*
Turning Miniatures in Wood	*John Sainsbury*
Turning Pens and Pencils	*Kip Christensen & Rex Burningham*
Understanding Woodturning	*Ann & Bob Phillips*
Useful Techniques for Woodturners	*GMC Publications*
Useful Woodturning Projects	*GMC Publications*

Woodturning: Bowls, Platters, Hollow Forms, Vases,	
Vessels, Bottles, Flasks, Tankards, Plates	*GMC Publications*
Woodturning: A Foundation Course (New Edition)	*Keith Rowley*
Woodturning: A Fresh Approach	*Robert Chapman*
Woodturning: An Individual Approach	*Dave Regester*
Woodturning: A Source Book of Shapes	*John Hunnex*
Woodturning Jewellery	*Hilary Bowen*
Woodturning Masterclass	*Tony Boase*
Woodturning Techniques	*GMC Publications*
Woodturning Tools & Equipment Test Reports	*GMC Publications*
Woodturning Wizardry	*David Springett*

WOODWORKING

Advanced Scrollsaw Projects	*GMC Publications*
Bird Boxes and Feeders for the Garden	*Dave Mackenzie*
Complete Woodfinishing	*Ian Hosker*
David Charlesworth's Furniture-Making Techniques	*David Charlesworth*
The Encyclopedia of Joint Making	*Terrie Noll*
Furniture & Cabinetmaking Projects	*GMC Publications*
Furniture-Making Projects for the Wood Craftsman	*GMC Publications*
Furniture-Making Techniques for the Wood Craftsman	*GMC Publications*
Furniture Projects	*Rod Wales*
Furniture Restoration (Practical Crafts)	*Kevin Jan Bonner*
Furniture Restoration and Repair for Beginners	*Kevin Jan Bonner*
Furniture Restoration Workshop	*Kevin Jan Bonner*
Green Woodwork	*Mike Abbott*
Kevin Ley's Furniture Projects	*Kevin Ley*
Making & Modifying Woodworking Tools	*Jim Kingshott*
Making Chairs and Tables	*GMC Publications*
Making Classic English Furniture	*Paul Richardson*
Making Little Boxes from Wood	*John Bennett*
Making Screw Threads in Wood	*Fred Holder*
Making Shaker Furniture	*Barry Jackson*
Making Woodwork Aids and Devices	*Robert Wearing*
Mastering the Router	*Ron Fox*
Minidrill: Fifteen Projects	*John Everett*
Pine Furniture Projects for the Home	*Dave Mackenzie*
Practical Scrollsaw Patterns	*John Everett*
Router Magic: Jigs, Fixtures and Tricks to	
Unleash your Router's Full Potential	*Bill Hylton*
Routing for Beginners	*Anthony Bailey*
The Scrollsaw: Twenty Projects	*John Everett*
Sharpening: The Complete Guide	*Jim Kingshott*
Sharpening Pocket Reference Book	*Jim Kingshott*
Simple Scrollsaw Projects	*GMC Publications*
Space-Saving Furniture Projects	*Dave Mackenzie*
Stickmaking: A Complete Course	*Andrew Jones & Clive George*
Stickmaking Handbook	*Andrew Jones & Clive George*
Test Reports: *The Router* and	
Furniture & Cabinetmaking	*GMC Publications*

GARDENING

PHOTOGRAPHY

VIDEOS

MAGAZINES

WOODTURNING ✦ WOODCARVING
FURNITURE & CABINETMAKING
THE ROUTER ✦ WOODWORKING
THE DOLLS' HOUSE MAGAZINE
WATER GARDENING
EXOTIC GARDENING
GARDEN CALENDAR
OUTDOOR PHOTOGRAPHY
BUSINESSMATTERS

The above represents a full list of all titles currently published or scheduled to be published.
All are available direct from the Publishers or through bookshops, newsagents and specialist retailers.
To place an order, or to obtain a complete catalogue, contact:

GMC Publications,
Castle Place, 166 High Street, Lewes, East Sussex BN7 1XU, United Kingdom
Tel: 01273 488005 Fax: 01273 478606
E-mail: pubs@thegmcgroup.com

Orders by credit card are accepted